DONATELLO

COMPLETE
PHAIDON EDITION

DONATELLO

Goldscheider, Ludwig

PHAIDON EDITION
OXFORD UNIVERSITY PRESS · NEW YORK

MADE IN GREAT BRITAIN

FIRST PRINTED 1941

24395

HARRISON & SONS LTD · 44-47 · ST. MARTIN'S LANE · LONDON · W.C.2

PRINTERS TO HIS MAJESTY THE KING

PREFACE

AFTER the Western Empire of Rome had succumbed before the inroad of the barbarians from the north and the east, the old civilization persisted in Byzantium and Gaul, to return thence, doubly modified, when the motherland had once more become hospitable. From Byzantium came scholars who could read, not only the Latin poets, but also the Greek philosophers, Plato and Aristotle; there came, too, artist-craftsmen, who knew how to cast bronze doors for the Italian cathedrals then in course of erection; who showed their colour-sense in enamels, silk embroideries, and the illumination of manuscripts; and who brought carved ivories that had preserved something of the spirit of Hellenic sculpture. Singers from Provence taught Dante and Petrarch new verbal cadences which would have been impossible unless Vergil and Catullus had written in antiquity; and it was from Apuleius and from French versifiers that Boccaccio learned his skill in story-telling. From Sicily, from the ancient Greek settlement upon Italian soil, from the court of Frederick II of Hohenstaufen, came the revival of the arts which gave the beauties of the classical world new forms. Provençals, Italians, and Germans, who constituted a primitive congregation of humanists upon the territory of this alien emperor, who were in search of the vanished greatness of Rome, and delved eagerly into the rich past as precursors of an even richer future. From Apulia to Tuscany came Nicola Pisano, the first sculptor of the Renaissance. Studying the reliefs of timeworn sarcophagi, he learned to how great an extent the human body could be the measure of all artistic things; his son Giovanni, who was completing the pulpit of the Siena cathedral, deliberately reproduced the plastic reliefs of Roman imperial days, and wittingly chiselled in accordance with the model specimens of Francisco-Roman art. His pupil Andrea Pisano brought these achievements from Pisa to Florence; he cast the first bronze door of the Florentine baptistry, whose areas are composed with the same tasteful sense of space as are the relief-images on ancient coins. This work gave Florence the primacy in sculpture for a century to come.

Florence, where Donatello was born, was older than Rome. It is usual to regard the city as having been primarily an Etruscan settlement. But about a thousand years before the Christian era this region was peopled by a race of different origin from the Etruscans, consisting of immigrants from the north. A feature common to the pre-Etruscan and the Etruscan civilization of this town was the love of bronze. From the tombs of early settlers have been excavated marvellous bronze helmets made to surmount cinerary urns, and also bronze figurines. To the period of the second settlement belong such masterpieces as the Arringatore and the Chimaera of Arezzo. Florence was still characterised in the days of the Renaissance by this taste for bronze, and also for such softer materials as clay and wax which may be used for models of bronze sculptures. Ghiberti, Donatello, Verrocchio, and Pollaiuolo all worked in bronze; and the Romans thought in marble.

Florence is an Etruscan town; the Etruscans were devoted to commerce and pleasure, and Florence remained a city of commerce and pleasure into the time of the Renaissance. The lords who were the masters of trade were the masters of the town as well. Before the Medici, the great speculators, rose to power, Florence was ruled by an oligarchy of wealthy mercantile families, and it was against this oligarchy that the populace rose in revolt in 1378, the movement being known to history as the "tumulto dei Ciompi". The rebellion was speedily suppressed, and many of the ringleaders took to flight. One of them, a wool-carder named Niccolò di Betto Bardi, removed to Pisa and thence to Lucca, where he once more became involved in political troubles. Rehabilitated after two years, he went back to Florence. This Niccolò di Betto Bardi was Donatello's father. He and his wife, Monna Orsa, lived in the San Pietro quarter at Gattolino, near what is now the Porta Romana.

Donatello, born in 1386, was of almost the same age as Fra Angelico and Jan van Eyck, and a few years younger than St. Bernardino of Siena and Thomas à Kempis. These four names typify the spirit of the time; in art the rediscovery of nature for the portrayal of man and landscape, and the laws of grandiose composition; and in religion a trend towards agitation and discipline. The days of mysticism were over. The previous generation had known Tauler and Ruysbroeck, Suso and Catherine of Siena;

but the new age held that supreme wisdom had been that of the pagan philosophers. Gone was the era of Byzantine and Gothic expressionist art, which accorded no more than a symbolical value to colour and line; of ecstatic art which, in front of golden backgrounds, glorified hideousness and sorrow: gone, too, were the arts of unaspiring detail-work and small-scale ivory folding-altars and illuminated initials. The new art aimed at the representation of external reality, at the reflection of heroic magnificence, at anatomical accuracy and the profundity of space, at corporeal substantiality. What was truly novel about it, what expressed its essentiality, was the use of central perspective, which was unknown to the classical epoch and to the Middle Ages. Perspective as a method of representation is a projection of individualism; the outer world is depicted in the way in which it makes itself subjectively known to us, not in the way in which it is objectively known to exist, with its relative magnitudes and the relative course of its lines. The next step in the individualisation of artistic representation is impressionism, which has recognised the relativity both of forms and of colours. Donatello's contemporaries, and among them his friend Paolo Uccello, put the finishing touches to perspective. Donatello's flat reliefs were the beginning of modern impressionism.

The artists of the Middle Ages were handicraftsmen assembled into a guild, for there was not as yet any sharp differentiation between arts and crafts. The Florentine workshop of the Pollaiuolo brothers (in the second half of the fifteenth century), was still a place where crafts were practised: sculpture of all kinds, goldsmith's work, bronze-founding, the making of buttons and small-arms, cutlery, paintings and copperplate engravings, designs for tapistry and stained-glass windows, domestic altars and medallions. Donatello himself was a master of many crafts; he learned goldsmith's work and how to make inlays, the application of stucco ornaments to furniture, the arts of painting and sculpture. In sculpture his teacher was Ghiberti, under whom he began to work at the age of seventeen, and whom he helped in the fashioning of the bronze doors for the baptistry. At twenty he laboured as stonemason on the Duomo of Florence. In 1412 he became a member of the painters' guild. At San Lorenzo in Florence, and during the building of the church of St. Anthony of Padua, he functioned as architect; and in fortifying Lucca he was one of the engineers.

But his supreme talent was sculpture, and considered from this aspect alone he was so multifarious that in the most diversified subsequent periods experts were able to find continually new reasons for admiration. His contemporaries were impressed, above all, by his unrivalled naturalness in the treatment of the nude. His bronze David was considered to have been cast from life. Especially extolled was the technical perfection of his big bronzes. Michelangelo copied Donatello's early works, and the latter's Martelli David, his statue of the seated John, and his Madonna upon the clouds, had a marked influence upon the former. Raphael was affected by Donatello's later advances in composition, and made sketches of his Paduan reliefs. Vasari praised him most of all as pioneer of mannerism and the baroque style; and for his group of Judith and Holofernes; but failed to understand those of his works that were still Gothic, like the bronze statue of St. Louis. In the epoch of the rococo, his putti and his Cupids were chiefly praised and imitated. The later classical epochs did not esteem him; neither Goethe nor Stendhal mentions Donatello in their respective accounts of their Italian journeys. It was not until towards the close of the nineteenth century that the historians of art rediscovered him. Courajod, Semper, and Bode were amazed by the naturalness of his cathedral prophets. Rodin enthusiastically acknowledged him to have been the ancestor of his own impressionism.

Donatello's first marble sculptures were chivalrous guardians, guarding law, freedom, and the city. The evangelists Mark and John (the former being a statue in front of the Florentine corn exchange, and the latter having originally been placed on the façade of the Duomo) are holding in their sinewy hands the books conveying the message that has been entrusted to them. They exhibit the faith in which heroism is rooted. With like unceasing calm does the Florentine lion support the shield with the arms of the town, while St. George holds the shield adorned with the symbol of peace. George is protected by nothing more than his cuirass and his inviolable courage; he has neither helmet nor sword, but we feel his steadfastness to be indomitable. Even sturdier, even more valiant, is the John on the western face of the Campanile, unfolding his scroll of manuscript like a herald who has a command to announce.

David, garlanded like a classical Bacchus, and with the head of Goliath at his feet, is a symbol of freedom, a symbol of youthful courage, undismayed by the seemingly invincible might of his giant adversary.

A young man contemplating the formidable head of such a terrific opponent is a classical theme. Consider, for instance, Perseus and Medusa. Donatello was fond of showing such a hideous sight as the head of a slain enemy. Four times he sculptured David with that of Goliath; and he took two other relevant tales from the Bible, twice showing Salome with the head of John the Baptist, and once showing Judith decapitating Holofernes. On the socle of this last bronze group is the primary classical symbol of the Gorgon's head.

The late Renaissance, which learned much from Donatello, recognised his *terribilità*, his aim at depicting that which is both stupendous and calculated to inspire fear, in a way equivalent to the shock-producing and carthartic effect of tragedy, this being contrasted with the Apollonian and epic tranquillity of Ghiberti, the lyrical amiability of Luca della Robbia, and the processional pomp of Verrocchio. Donatello's taste for the tragical and dramatic is also to be understood literally: the scenes of his Salome reliefs with their numerous architectonic glimpses seem to depict happenings in the theatre; his John reliefs in San Lorenzo remind us of the striking development of mystery plays; and his one big bronze relief in Padua, the healing of the hot-tempered young man, is staged in a tennis-court—in such an arena as that which the early Renaissance was actually wont to use for religious dramas.

Donatello's tragical pathos is shown by some of his other works, such as the Scourging, the Crucifixion, and the Deploration of Jesus; the savage lineaments of his figures of John the Baptist and those of his cathedral prophets; the witchlike Mary Magdalene; and the corpse of a peasant soldier who has been nailed on the cross as representative of Christ. His martyrs and apostles in the reliefs on the bronze doors are heroes, are (as his contemporary Filarete remarked) "not sufferers but fighters". In the equestrian statue before the Santo he produced a perfect symbol of the heroic, mightier than anything achieved by the Romans.

Nevertheless Donatello was pre-eminently the sculptor of the delicate and the cheerful. The symbol he uses to denote the innocence and merriment of life is the nude body of a child, the putto, which is given a place in almost all his works. His Prato pulpit and his Florentine choir galleries are entirely fashioned of white putti against a golden ground; he shows putti upon the cover of the Sienese font; tottering they bear the crown of victory at the feet of the champion St. George; he has sculptured them as ornaments of fountains and as candlesticks; they support the body of the dead Christ; they have places above the altar of the Annunciation; behind the Virgin and the Child they stand as angels; as musicians they are among the dark figures of the Paduan high altar; at the vintage they gather the grapes and tread them, they celebrate their bacchanal upon the socle of the Judith. They appear, likewise, where we should never have expected them; in the frieze above the solemn scenes of the San Lorenzo pulpits; on the episcopal staff of St. Louis; on Goliath's helmet at the feet of the bronze David; and on the saddle of the formidable Gattamelata. Donatello's art had all the span of supreme drama, where merriment treads upon the heels of mourning—in a word, it had all the comprehensiveness of life.

Donatello worked in four towns: in Florence, the city of secular rule, of gain and possession, the city of merchants; in Rome, the city of religious dominion, of the heirs of the Caesars, of the Popes and the Princes of the Church; in Siena, the town of faith and enthusiasm, of the mystics and the ascetics; and in Padua, the headquarters of a humanist university, the shrine of testing and of knowledge. No less diversified than the scenes in which the eighty years of Donatello's life were spent, were the times he traversed. When he was born, Petrarch and Boccaccio had been dead no more than ten years; when he died, Leonardo was already fourteen years old. During these eight decades, much had happened in Florence and elsewhere: Cosimo de' Medici had become master of the town upon the Arno, where his grandson Lorenzo the Magnificent had succeeded him; at the Platonic Academy of the Medici, the humanists spelled out their Greek classics until, after the fall of Constantinople, Greek scholars fled to Rome and Florence, bringing more abundant knowledge; Brunelleschi had built the dome of the cathedral; in distant lands John Huss had been burned and also Joan of Arc; in Rome Bernardino of Siena had preached, and had made a bonfire of the vanities of the world; the plague had raged in the city; the exile of the Popes had long since come to an end, the building of the Vatican Library and the reconstruction of St. Peter's had been begun; Aeneas Sylvius Piccolomini, a much travelled man and an able poet, who surrounded himself with humanists, had occupied the papal throne as Pius II; to be followed by Paul II, a great collector of art treasures and a distinguished man of the world, who introduced carnival festivities into Rome and horse-races upon the Corso. Donatello's life opened upon the border of the Gothic age, and ended when the modern epoch had well begun.

Portrait of Donatello. Detail from a fresco painting by Vasari
Florence, Palazzo Vecchio.

This life was wholly devoted to work; we have no information about his private concerns, not even so much as a letter or a drawing. We know that Donatello's father died when the boy was very young, and his mother when he was in the middle forties; he had lived with her till then, having never married. In Rome he and his friend Brunelleschi "dug for treasure", which really meant that they made excavations in search of vestiges of classical architecture and sculpture; this happening at a time when the Laocoon and the Apollo Belvedere were still hidden under heaps of rubbish. He was poor, but (if we are to believe Vasari) generous in money matters. Having been trained in the Stonemasons' Guild, he did not, like Michelangelo, care to work singlehanded, but was always surrounded by assistants. In Padua he had twenty of these; while, when working on the San Lorenzo pulpits, he had a number who were both young and talented, among them being Riccio and Bertoldo. Vasari tells us that Cosimo de' Medici gave him a red cloak, and Piero a vineyard, but that he returned both these gifts, not knowing what to make of them. In his closing years he was bedridden and paralysed. He died on December 13, 1466, and was buried in the crypt of San Lorenzo, close to Cosimo de' Medici.

When he had passed away there was a reaction in the art and craft of Florentine sculpture; people began to make coloured and glazed terracotta images, decorative portraits, small ornate bronzes, virtuoso monuments. The work had all grown too easy. Donatello and his assistants had shown how to make bronze castings; how a block of stone, when it had been chiselled, could still preserve the aspect of a block; how a relief containing numerous figures could be composed; how it could be worked so flat that it had the charm of a drawing, and how movement could be represented. The power of technique had become common to all sculptors, and they could carry technique a stage farther on. What was still unattainable by them was Donatello's expressive power, which had been that of a man in whom an inborn talent finds vent—the vigour of a genius who can disregard all that has been tried and done before, can shake it off as he would shake the dust from off his feet on leaving a foreign city, to begin over again from the very beginning.

LONDON, JANUARY, 1941   LUDWIG GOLDSCHEIDER

(The appended systematic account of the whole of Donatello's creative work deals with all he ever produced, including what has been lost as well as what has come down to us. Mention is likewise made of other important works that proceeded from his studio, the names of his assistants being given in each case. The reference to the literature of the subject that accompany the brief catalogue will make it easy for the student to trace the sources of information and to gain an adequate insight into this field of research. Measurements that are lacking in previous monographs on Donatello have been furnished. The figures in the margins relate to the photogravure plates of the present volume.)

We have very little information about the early days of Donatello, but we can make some likely guesses by piecing together various confused data recorded by Vasari. Thus, in his account of the life of Lorenzo di Bicci, Vasari tells us that Donatello, "being then quite young", assisted Bicci in the painting of the frescoes on the façade of the cloister of Santa Croce, the subjects dealt with being the Assumption of the Blessed Virgin and the Madonna giving her girdle to St. Thomas. Lorenzo di Bicci was associated with Florentine sculpture, having (as did Agnolo di Gaddi and Spinello Aretino) provided plans for the sculptures of the Duomo, and also models for the figures of the saints by Piero di Giovanni in the Medici Palace. It seems possible, therefore, that for a time Donatello may have been one of Lorenzo di Bicci's pupils. —Vasari reports at considerable length that Donatello collaborated with Nanni di Banco in sculpturing the latter's *Quattro Coronati* (the Four Holy Sculptors),[1]

---

[1] Vasari's assertion that Nanni di Banco was Donatello's pupil must, of course, be interpreted by contraries, as the former was much older (1373–1420). Even so, there is no evidence that Donatello was his pupil, but in view of the characteristics of Donatello's early work the contention might be defended.

FIG. 2.—*Filippo Brunelleschi : The Sacrificing of Isaac. Bronze. Florence, Bargello*

and that Donatello showed how to overcome the difficulty of finding room for the four figures in a narrow niche (Fig. 1). How closely linked was Donatello in his early sculptures with Nanni di Banco is shown by the fact that, whereas by Schottmüller and Schubring the St. Peter on the Or San Michele (Fig. 6) is regarded as the work of the latter, it is by Wulff and Kauffmann ascribed to Donatello. Nor, then, can we reject the idea that Donatello, who certainly gave much help in the sculptural adornment of the Or San Michele, may have contributed to Nanni di Banco's *Quattro Coronati.*—We learn also from Vasari that Donatello participated in the competition for the second pair of bronze gates for the Baptistry at Florence (1401–1402). Donatello's design, says Vasari, "was excellent, but not sufficiently well executed". Ghiberti, in his autobiography, does not mention Donatello as one of the competitors. The theme for the competition was the *Sacrificing of Isaac*, and the two reliefs by Ghiberti and Brunelleschi (Fig. 2) are preserved. Vasari's account may mean that Donatello helped in producing Brunelleschi's design. Anyhow, they both agreed in

FIG. 1.—*Nanni di Banco : Quattro Coronati. Marble. Florence, Or San Michele*

regarding Ghiberti's as preferable, and to Ghiberti the erection of the second pair of bronze gates was entrusted.—The friendship between Brunelleschi and Donatello—a much younger man[2]—lasted four decades. They worked together a good many times, last of all upon the decoration of the sacristy of the church of San Lorenzo (towards 1440). Vasari and the anonymous biographer of Brunelleschi[3] both allude to a first journey to Rome made together by Donatello and Brunelleschi, but of this we have no trustworthy records. On this

theory the date would be 1402–1403.[4] In November, 1403, Donatello was unquestionably an assistant in Ghiberti's studio, as he was again in 1407 when he already had some independent commissions for the sculptures on the Duomo. Ciuffagni and Michelozzo worked for a while in the same studio, later becoming collaborators with Donatello; another fellow-assistant at Ghiberti's was Paolo Uzzano, the painter, with whom Donatello was on friendly terms. It is generally supposed that at Ghiberti's workshop Donatello was concerned, not so much with helping to prepare the reliefs on the bronze gate of the Baptistry, as with a goldsmith's job.—Further information concerning the craftsmanship of young Donatello is given by Vasari in his life of the Florentine painter, Dello Delli: "Dello painted the entire furniture of a chamber for Giovanni de' Medici; a work which was then considered of rare excellence. . . . It is said that our artist was aided in this work by Donatello, then a boy, who made him various ornaments, and even

[2] Some documents give the year of Donatello's birth as 1386, others as 1383 or 1382 (H. Semper, *Quellenschriften für Kunstgeschichte*, IX, Vienna 1875, pp. 231 and foll.). Filippo Brunelleschi was born in 1377 and died in 1446. It is remarkable that Vasari (just as he did in the case of Nanni di Banco) should make out that the older artist, Brunelleschi, was a pupil of the younger one: "Filippo was seized with an earnest desire to attempt the art of sculpture, and this took effect in such sort that Donatello, then a youth, being considered of great distinction and high promise therein, Filippo entered into close intimacy with him, and, each attracted by the talents of the other, they became so strongly attached that one seemed unable to live without the other". Famous has become Vasari's story of the rivalry between the two artists which is supposed to have led to the carving of the two wooden crucifixes, Donatello's in the church of Santa Croce, and Brunelleschi's in the church of Santa Maria Novella; but Brunelleschi's crucifix must have been made twenty years later than Donatello's.

[3] Moreni's edition, 1812; H. Holtzinger's edition, Stuttgart 1886.

[4] H. Heydenreich, "Jahrb. d. preuss. Kunstsammlungen", LII, 1931, pp. 8 and foll.; and G. de Franchovich, "Boll. d'arte", IX, 1929, pp. 146 and foll.

FIGS. 3–4.—*Donatello: Two Prophets. Marble. 1406–1408. Florence Duomo Porta Mandorla*

FIG. 5.—*Attributed to Donatello: Madonna and Child. Marble. Berlin Kaiser-Friedrich-Museum* stories, in bas-relief, formed of stucco, chalk, glue, and pounded bricks, which, being gilded, served as a rich and beautiful accompaniment to the paintings". Beyond question, Donatello exercised various other crafts beside that of sculptor, being painter, engraver of medals, goldsmith, intaglio-carver, and architect. (Records of the Operai del Duomo, for March, 18, 1436: "Aurifex et magister intagli.")

On November 23, 1406, Donatello's name appears for the first time in the Records of the Masonic Artists who worked upon the Duomo; the next entry being on February 17, 1408. The payments relate to THE TWO STATUETTES OF THE PROPHETS ABOVE THE PORTA MANDORLA (Figs. 3 and 4). They are of marble, about 2 ft. 10 in. high. The left one is the earlier of the two, and its feet are not completely finished; the right one has

FIG. 6.—*Nanni di Banco (or Donatello ?): St. Peter. Marble. About 1412.*
Florence, Or San Michele

FIG. 7.—*Donatello: St. Mark. 1412. Florence, Or San Michele.*
(Cf. Plates 7 and 8.)

been fixed leaning slightly forward.[5] The head of a prophet and the head of a sibyl of a much later date (1422) on the hood-moulding of the Porta Mandorla come from Donatello's studio.[6] A MADONNA STATUETTE IN THE BERLIN MUSEUM (Inv. No. 2016) was considered by Wilhelm von Bode to have been an early work of Donatello's (about 1408–1410): Schubring agrees in ascribing this insignificant carving to Donatello (Fig. 5). The statuette has been stored away, and no longer appears in the 1933 catalogue.—The DAVID OF THE BARGELLO (marble, height 6 ft. 3½ in.) comes from the Palazzo Vecchio, but is supposed to have been intended to stand upon the buttress of a chapel in the Duomo. The sling of silk or bronze which David must have held in his right hand has been lost. The strangely extended position of the left arm and the left hand has classical prototypes (cf. bronze tripod from Pompeii with three Pan figures, Museo Nazionale of Naples; J. Sieveking, *Antike Metallgeräte*, Pl. XVII).—During the period 1410–1412 Donatello completed a statue of Joshua, which has been lost.—The ST. MARK of Or San Michele (marble, height about 7 ft.) was a commission from the Joiners' Guild;[7] the ST. PETER (Fig. 6) was made to order for the Butcher's Guild. The St. Mark is especially characterised by contrasts; by a marked insistence upon the difference between the working leg and the idle leg; by the advanced position of the left shoulder; and by the artistic asymmetry of the folds of the clothing. Among the numerous almost bodiless statues for the guild-niches of Or San Michele, the St. Mark impresses us by its size and its massive strength. Michelangelo's St. Peter on the Piccolomini altar at Siena is a faint reproduction of Donatello's St. Mark; but even Michelangelo's monumental David shows in its vivid contraposition how great an influence the earlier master had upon the later. Incorporeal, on the other hand, seems the St. Peter, with its drooping and flapping vestments, its lack of statics, its petty amorphousness; for only the head displays a certain amount of vigour. There is reason to erase this statue from the list of Donatello's works, despite Wulff (Donatello, Leipzig, 1922, p. 4) and Schubring (II, p. 40). Kauffmann

(p. 50), too, considers it to be Donatello's, but believes that Brunelleschi may have collaborated.

In the year 1408 three blocks of marble were respectively assigned to Niccolò d'Arezzo, Nanni di Banco, and Donatello; in 1410, a fourth block to Ciuffagni.[8] The first payment to Donatello was made in 1413, the last in October, 1415. The four blocks of marble were intended for seated statues of the evangelists on the façade of the Duomo. There they remained till 1587; then they were removed to the choir of the Duomo; but since 1904 they have been in the aisles—Donatello's ST. JOHN in the southern aisle, beside Niccolò's d'Arezzo weak St. Mark. The statue, which is over life-size, was hewn out of a rather shallow block. To leave sufficient marble for the thighs of the seated figure, Donatello sculptured the upper part of the body as a high relief, omitting the back.

FIGS. 8–10.—*Heads of Apostles and Evangelists, 14th Century.*
8.—German; Münster, Notre-Dame.
9.—Italian; Donatello (cf. Pl. 9).
10.—French; Ghent, Museum (cf. Pl. 10).

The Guild of Armourers (corazzai e spadai) commissioned Donatello with the statue of ST. GEORGE for one of the guild niches at Or San Michele (marble, 6 ft. 9 in. high). The original is now in the Bargello, while where it used to stand there is a bronze copy. Lord Balcarres writes (pp. 39–42): "The St. George is the most famous of Donatello's statues, and is generally called his masterpiece. . . . In some ways it spoke the last word; closed an episode in the history of art." Whole books have been devoted to it, that of Bocchi in 1571 and that of W. F. Volbach in 1917. The statue has been compared with those of Lysippus and with those of the Gothic cathedrals. The tip of the nose is a modern restoration, having been broken off in 1858 by a thrown stone.—The marble socle-relief (Fig. 11) on the niche of the St. George at Or San Michele, showing ST. GEORGE AND THE DRAGON (16 in. by 48 in.), is generally considered to date from

---

[5] *Reliquiae Wottonianae*, by Sir Henry Wotton, 4th edition, London, 1665, pp. 61 and foll.: " That in placing of standing figures aloft, we must set them in a posture somewhat bowing forward, because (saith our Master Vitruvius, lib 3, cap. 3, out of a better art than his own) the visual beam of our eye, extended to the head of the said figures, being longer than to the foot, must necessarily make that part appear farther; so to reduce it to an erect or upright position, there must be allowed a due advantage of stooping towards us, which Albert Dürer hath exactly taught in his forementioned Geometry. Our Vitruvius calleth this affection in the eye a resupination of the figure." We see that the optical principles applied by Donatello were already used in antiquity.

[6] Kauffmann, p. 32; p. 223, note 252.

[7] Vasari writes: " The figure of St. Mark was undertaken in the first instance in concert with Filippo Brunelleschi for the Joiners' Guild, but, with Filippo's consent, was ultimately finished by Donatello unaided ". This collaboration with Brunelleschi was interpreted as for the St. Peter.

[8] Bernardo Ciuffagni (1381–1457) and Donatello were Ghiberti's assistants in the making of the latter's first bronze gate (the second bronze gate of the Baptistry). In 1417 Ciuffagni did some work on a Joshua for the Campanile, but never finished it. According to Bode (*Toskanische Bildhauer*, p. 15), it was finished in 1421 by Donatello and Rossi. From 1422 onward, Ciuffagni was again working for the Duomo of Florence, as an imitator of Donatello. Cf. Semper, p. 77, as to a supposed collaboration between Niccolò d'Arezzo and Donatello.

about 1416, but the view that it originated contemporaneously with the Brancacci-Relief (Pl. 70) is more likely to be correct. Eric Maclagan (*Italian Sculpture in the Victoria and Albert Museum*, 1932, p. 19) writes : " The Marble Relief is usually ascribed to the same early period, about 1416, as the statue of St. George, which stood formerly in the niche above it (now in the Bargello), but it may well belong to the same period as the following reliefs " (*cf*. Pl. 72 and Fig. 56) " about 1430 ". This relief is made peculiarly interesting by its markedly impressionist style, which is most conspicuous in the mountain and forest landscape of the background.

FIGS. 11–13.—*St. George and the Dragon.*
11.—*Marble Relief by Donatello. Niche of St. George, outside Or San Michele at Florence.*
12.—*Relief in Stucco, after the original marble. London, Victoria and Albert Museum.*
13.—*Marble Relief by Michel Colombe, 1508. Paris, Louvre*

In the London stucco reproduction (shown in Fig. 12), the landscape can be better discerned than in the original, which has been damaged. How strongly developed Donatello's impressionism was can be best learned by a comparison of Fig. 12 with Fig. 13, which represents a kindred composition in relief, dated from about eighty years later, by a French master.

The MARZOCCO, the armorial lion that originally stood sentinel in a courtyard of Santa Maria Novella, on the staircase leading to the " Papal Quarters ", was probably (as Schubring was the first to point out) a quasi-representation of the lions kept in the dungeons of the palace. The animals were carefully observed in times of crisis, and their demeanour was supposed to give oracular information. Pope Martin V visited Florence in 1419, and the Marzocco may have been designed as a preliminary to his reception. It was placed in position in February, 1420 (Semper, p. 278 ; Kauffmann, note 112). Originally the statue wore a crown, probably of bronze. The socle, which is decorated with the armorial bearings assigned in 1452 to Jean Count of Dunois, is not the work of Donatello. On this socle, which in 1810 was transferred from Santa Maria Novella to the front of the Palazzo Vecchio, there now stands a bronze replica of the Marzocco, the original having been brought for safe keeping to the Bargello of the National Museum. Akin to this lion known as the Marzocco, and bearing the Florentine arms, is the winged lion on the socle of the tabernacle of St. Mark. (Or San Michele, *see* Fig. 7.)

FIG. 14.—*Donatello : The Martelli Shield. Tinted Marble. About 1430–1432. Florence, Casa Martelli*

Vasari tells us that Donatello sculptured other ARMORIAL BEARINGS: "He frequently executed the arms of families; for example, placing them over the chimney-pieces, or on the fronts of the houses of the citizens." Bocchi (1571) mentions the arms of the Pazzi, the Becchi, and the Boni among the works of Donatello. Yet another coat of arms which has previously escaped notice is discussed by Wilhelm Valentiner ("Art News", 1928, pp. 15 and foll.). Apart from numerous coats of arms that have been unwarrantably ascribed to Donatello (Balcarres, p. 68; illustrations, Schubring, pp. 189, 210 and 219), we should specially refer to the MARTELLI SHIELD, which Schubring speaks of as "the finest of Italian armorial bearings" (Fig. 14). Balcarres points out that the winged griffin rampant on this shield can be classed with the Etruscan Chimaera of Arezzo.

18–22 The outsize WOODEN CRUCIFIX was Donatello's first commission from a private person—probably belonging to the Barbigia family. As Kauffmann showed (note 44), the arms of the Crucifix were rotatory, no doubt in order that during a mystery play the sculptured figure

FIG. 16.—*Second Storey of the Campanile, West Side; with three statues by Donatello: St. John the Baptist, Zuccone and Jeremiah; and the Obadiah by Rosso*

could be taken down from the cross and laid in the tomb. Traces of the old bright tinting can be discerned in the shroud, and therefore we can infer that beneath the brown overlay which covers the rest of the figure the original vivid colours exist.

Towards the end of 1415 began Donatello's commissions for THE STATUES OF THE CAMPANILE, on which he continued to work for twenty years (Figs. 15 and 16). Of the sixteen statues that decorate the second storey of the Campanile (the bell-tower of the Duomo), three are certainly Donatello's, while two others have sometimes been ascribed to him, and the figures of the Abraham and Isaac group were the joint work of Donatello and Rosso. The statues are of marble, and range from 6 ft. 6 in. to 7 ft. in height. Donatello's are the JOHN, the JEREMIAH, and the ZUCCONE, this being incontrovertibly proved by the signature "opus Donatelli". The trecento socles on which they stand and the names of "David Rex" and "Salomon Rex" are of no importance. As regards the John, Schubring opines (pp. 14 and 194) that it rather should be called Jonah. The statues of Jeremiah and Job (Il Zuccone) have always been regarded as portraits, and, indeed, though confirmation is lacking, as likenesses of Francesco Soderini and Barduccio Cherichini. The John gives the impression of being an advance upon the St. George; the Jeremiah and the Zuccone are among Donatello's most splendid creations, and detailed description of these three is needless, since we were able on a scaffolding 60 ft. high to secure close-up photographs of them (*see* Plates 26, 46 to 52).—To what extent Donatello's naturalism was a brilliant innovation, and to what extent a product of his time, cannot be ascertained by comparing his works with those of his Italian contemporaries, but it can by comparing them with Nordic sculptures: Donatello seems more akin to Claus Sluter the elder, a Dutchman

26–
44–
49–

FIG. 15.—*The Campanile of the Duomo Santa Maria del Fiore in Florence, c. 280 feet high. Built by Giotto and followers, 1334–1387*

FIG. 17.—*The Prophet Isaiah. From the Fount in Champmol, near Dijon.*
By Claus Sluter. About 1396

MOSES (Fig. 19) was begun by Ciuffagni, and was mainly finished by Rosso.[9] Kauffmann considers that " the thinker's attitude of this figure, which so admirably unites head and hands into a picture of concentrated reflectiveness, was fit to inspire Raphael and Michelangelo," but he doubts whether Donatello had a hand in the work (pp. 22 and 36).—The ABRAHAM AND ISAAC GROUP (Fig. 20) is confirmed as the joint creation

FIG. 20.—*Donatello and Rosso: Abraham and Isaac. Marble. 1421.*
East side of the Campanile

who worked in Burgundy, than to any of his own fellow-countrymen (*cf.* Plate 50 and Fig. 17).—Of the Campanile statues the HABBAKUK (Fig. 18) has also been ascribed to Donatello—of late by Kauffmann (p. 26).   The so-called

FIG. 18.—*Hoary Prophet (so-called Habbakuk).* FIG. 19.—*Moses (or Joshua ?). About 1418.*
Marble. 1415–1422. Attributed to Donatello.   Joint work of Ciuffagni, Rosso and Donatello.
East side of the Campanile

of Donatello and Rosso.   Apart from his general share in the composition, it would appear that Donatello must have been chiefly responsible for the work upon Abraham's head and arms.   Michelangelo's unfinished *Matthew* (Florence, the Academy), with its vigorous

[9] Giovanni (Nani) di Bartolo, known as Il Rosso, worked for the Duomo of Florence from 1419 to 1422 as Donatello's assistant, or in conjunction with him. Obadiah (1422), in a niche on the western side of the Campanile, is signed by Rosso.   Later he worked at Verona, Venice, and Tolentino.   The equestrian statue that surmounts the sarcophagus of the condottiere Sarego in the church of Sant Anastasia at Verona (1424–1429) is interesting, were it only as a precursor of Donatello's " Gattamelata ".   The relief in the corner by the entrance to the Doges' Palace in Venice, " The Judgment of Solomon ", has been ascribed to him.   The precise dates of his birth and death are unknown. The former was about 1390, and the latter after 1451.

turning of head and shoulder, owes more to this Abraham than to the classical *Pasquino* (Rome).—The

23–25 prophet usually spoken of as the POGGIO BRACCIOLINI was not intended for the Campanile, but (like the *St. John* shown in Pl. 9) for the façade of the Duomo. Documents prove that Rosso was commissioned to do this work, but he had the permission to use the assistance of another master. Many authorities deny that Donatello had anything to do with the matter. G. Poggi ascribes the "Poggio Bracciolini" to Giuliano di Giovanni. The statue consists of two parts: the head and neck were separately sculptured, and attached to the clothed body. "The head was the work of Donatello, and the head was the chief merit of the Poggio, so that tradition rightly attaches to it the name of Donatello" (Kauffmann, p. 35). In any case we are dealing with a portrait statue; and some of the characteristics suggest, indeed, that a death-mask may have been used as model. Certainly the Poggio head has little in common with the three Campanile statues that were indubitably sculptured by Donatello; the hard treatment of the hair and of the folds at the angles of the eyes and the mouth have no resemblance to the well-known technique of Donatello (*cf.* Balcarres, p. 12).

31–33 In the time of Vasari, from 1463 onward, the bronze statue of ST. LOUIS (8 ft. 4 in.) stood in a niche above the main door of the church of Santa Croce in Florence. Schmarsow (1886), Semper (1887), and Semrau (1891) believed it to be a late work of Donatello's, dating from between 1440 and 1453. Since Meyer (1904) and Balcarres (1903), it has been generally believed that this statue must be the one which the Guelphs commissioned for a niche at Or San Michele, and which was completed in 1423. (*See* Kauffmann, p. 27 and note 77; Schubring, p. 23, and II, p. 43; Knapp, *Italienische Plastik*, Munich, 1923, p. 76; but *cf.* also Curt Sachs, 1904, and Bertaux, 1911). The statue is now exhibited in a good light in the Museo dell' Opera di Santa Croce. Conspicuous are the vestiges of gilding. A part of the back is wanting, as this figure was intended for a niche, and could therefore not be seen from behind. It was Donatello's first work in bronze, and Michelozzo[10] helped in the casting.

---

[10] Michelozzo Michelozzi (Michelozzo di Bartolomeo di Gherardo), sculptor and architect, was born in Florence towards 1396 and died in 1472. Michelozzo was court artist to Cosimo de' Medici, for whom he built monasteries and palaces (the cloisters of St. Mark and Santa Croce, the Palazzo Riccardi, the reconstruction of the Sforza Palace in Milan as a banking-house for the Medici, the adaptation of the Palazzo Vecchio, etc.). Accompanying Cosimo into exile, he visited Padua, Venice, and Dalmatia. As sculptor he collaborated with three great masters—Ghiberti, Luca della Robbia, and Donatello: he helped Ghiberti in the statue of St. Matthew and in the gates of the Baptistry; Luca della Robbia in the bronze statues of the two sacristies of the Duomo. From 1423 to 1438 he worked in Donatello's studio, collaborating in the bronze figure of St. Louis (Pl. 31 and Fig. 21), the tomb of Baldassare Coscia (Pope John XXIII, Fig. 26), the Brancacci monument (Fig. 27), the casting of the Salome relief and the other bronzes for Siena, the outer pulpit of the Prato Cathedral (Fig. 63), and the bronze bust of St. Rossore (Fig. 24). He was particularly useful to Donatello owing to his skill as bronze-founder.

FIG. 21.—*Andrea del Verrocchio: Christ and St. Thomas. Bronze. 1483. The tabernacle by Donatello and Michelozzo. 1423–1426. Florence, Or San Michele*

THE TABERNACLE OF THE PARTE GUELFA (marble, about 8 ft. by 19 ft.) originally intended for the bronze statue of St. Louis, now shelters Verrocchio's bronze group of Jesus and Doubting Thomas (Fig. 21). Curt Sachs (*Das Tabernakel mit Andrea del Verrocchios Thomasgruppe an Or San Michele zu Florenz*, Strassburg 1904, *Zur Kunstgeschichte des Auslandes*, Vol. XXIII) has critically studied this tabernacle. He considers that the entablature dates from about 1460, and that the heads on the socle must have been added (or renovated) in the cinquecento. But the right-hand mask is certainly part of the original work, not having been superposed but sculptured out of the primary block (Colasanti, pp. 43 and foll.; Kauffmann, note 316). The relief in the medallion on the pediment showing the Holy Trinity is, with its lively and impressive forms, obviously Donatello's work, this view being confirmed by an examination of Michelozzo's replica over a door of the Palazzetto di Parte Guelfa (Photo Alinari 3051A), where the ornamental characteristics of Michelozzo's work contrast typically with Donatello's naturalism.

The bronze statuette of JOHN THE BAPTIST (2 ft. 9 in.) was according to Bode ("Jahrb. d. Zeitschr. f. bild. Kunst," New Series, XVI, 1905, pp. 123 and foll.), originally designed for the font of the Baptistry at Orvieto (Fig. 22). According to the catalogue of the Berlin Museum

FIG. 22.—*Donatello: St. John the Baptist.*   FIG. 23.—*School of Donatello: St. John the*
Bronze Statuette. 1423. Berlin,   *Baptist. Bronze Statuette.*
Kaiser Friedrich Museum   *Paris, Louvre*

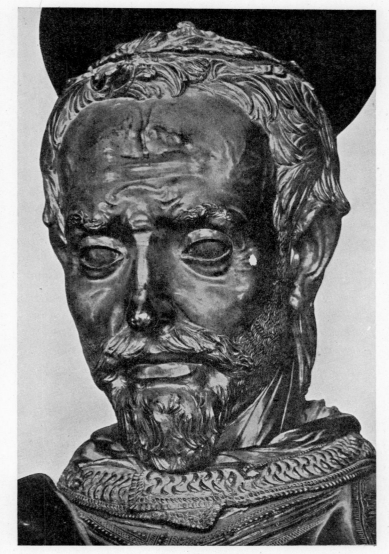

FIG. 24.—*Attributed to Donatello: St. Rossore. Reliquary, Silver-plated Copper. 1427.*
Pisa, S. Stefano

(*Bronzestatuetten*, 4th edition, 1930, No. 23), the left forearm of the statuette has been broken off and awkwardly replaced, while Kauffmann (note 96) declares that both the forearms are additions of a later date. Colosanti (p. 20) denies that the figure has any connexion with the font of Orvieto, and thinks it possible that we are concerned with a cast subsequently made from an independent model. As Meyer pointed out (p. 32), the statuette bears unmistakeable signs of defective casting, for there are holes and flaws, and probably the forearms were a failure.

THE ROSSORE RELIQUARY (Fig. 24) is doubted to be Donatello's work (Middeldorf, Burlington Mag., LIV, 1929, p. 188). Schubring (p. 201, text to Fig. on p. 170) considers it to have been executed by Michelozzo, after a model by Donatello. Kauffmann (note 97) favours the idea that this reliquary is really Donatello's work. It consists of two parts, and the head, which is loosely attached to the bust, produces a more favourable impression than the latter. The work, having been since 1427 at the Ognissanti church in Florence, was in 1592 removed to Pisa (Colasanti, p. 24).

There are also grave reasons for doubting whether the marble relief of THE SCOURGING OF JESUS in Berlin (1 ft. 6¼ in. by 1 ft. 10¾ in., Fig. 25) can have been Donatello's work, though Bode held that it was, and Bode's view has been generally accepted (last of all by Colasanti, p. 45); even Kauffmann agrees, though dubiously, and with some reserve (note 179). Folnesic ("Monatshefte f. Kunstwiss.", VIII, 1915, p. 190) ascribes the relief to a pupil of Giorgio da Sebenico named Niccolò Coccari,

who down to 1449 worked at Padua as Donatello's assistant, and then returned to his home in Dalmatia.

We now come to the MORTUARY MONUMENTS sculptured by Donatello, beginning with the TOMB OF BALDASSARE COSCIA, POPE JOHN XXIII (Fig. 26). It is believed that Donatello made the bronze statue of the Pope (Fig. 28);

30

FIG. 25.—*Attributed to Donatello: The Scourging of Christ. Marble Relief.*
About 1425 (?). Berlin, Kaiser-Friedrich Museum

FIG. 28.—*Donatello : Effigy of Pope John XXIII. Bronze. 1425–1427.*
Florence, Baptistery

Michelozzo the marble architecture of the tomb ; Pagno di Lapo Portigiani,[11] perhaps, the Madonna. (*See* Fabriczy, " Jahrb. d. preuss. Kunstsamml." 1894, pp. 247 and foll.) The TOMB OF CARDINAL BRANCACCI (Fig. 27) was executed in Pisa by Donatello and Michelozzo ; the Madonna was sculptured by Isaia da Pisa, who later executed the monument of Pope Eugenius IV in Rome (Schubring, p. 196). The ASSUNTA RELIEF (1 ft. 8¾ in. by 2 ft. 6¾ in.) on the sarcophagus of the Brancacci monument was Donatello's work, though perhaps Michelozzo assisted. Simultaneously with the Brancacci monument

was executed the bronze plate for the TOMB OF GIOVANNI PECCI, one of Donatello's signed works (Fig. 29). How much Donatello was influenced by Quercia is shown by a comparison of the latter's Trenta Tombstone (Fig. 31) with Donatello's SEPULCHRAL SLAB OF GIOVANNI CRIVELLI (Fig. 30), executed during the master's stay in Rome, and found in the church of Santa Maria in the Ara Coeli. Donatello was summoned to Rome in 1432 to appraise and improve Simone Ghini's[12] model for the TOMB OF POPE MARTIN V in the church of San Giovanni Laterano (Fig. 32). It is generally believed that this sepulchral plate (8 ft. 2 in. by 3 ft. 6 in.) is mainly the work of Donatello, and that apart from the actual casting only the ornamentation, the

---

[11] Pagno di Lapo Portigiani of Fiesole (1408–1471) became, at the age of 18, Donatello's and Michelozzo's assistant, continuing this work from 1426–1428. During 1428 he was Quercia's collaborator upon the Sienese font, and from 1434–1438 he participated in the sculpturing of Donatello's external pulpit for the cathedral of Prato. His principal plastic was the Madonna in the museum of the Florentine Operai del Duomo (1451).

[12] Vasari writes : " It is said that Simone, the brother of Donato, having prepared the model for the sepulchral monument of Pope Martia V, sent for Donato, to the end that he might see it before it should be cast ". Simone was not the brother of Donato (Donatello), but a friend ; probably nothing more than a bronze-founder. Vasari reports that several of his bronzes went to France, and speaks of other works as follows : " For the baptismal font of the Cathedral of Arezzo this master executed certain stories in bas-relief representing the Saviour being baptised by St. John ". The reliefs of the font in the Cathedral of Arezzo were ascribed to Donatello himself by Alessandro del Vita (*cf. I Duomo d'Arezzo*, pp. 48 and foll.) and by Frida Schottmüller (" Monatshefte f. Kunstwissenschaft ", II, 1909, p. 39). In this matter Vasari has made a mistake, failing to distinguish between Simone Ghini, who cast the sepulchral plate of Pope Martin V, and Simone di Nanni Ferrucci. To this Simone Ferrucci of Fiesole have been ascribed figures of the Virtues in the Church of St. Francis at Rimini, and a Madonna relief in the church of St. Dominic at Bologna, as well as a marble relief, the Baptism of Jesus, in Berlin (No. 7209). It is probable that a relief in the Ducal Palace at Mantua, showing Christ and two angels with the instruments of torture, is of the same workmanship as the reliefs on the Arezzo font (Photo Alinari, No. 18815).

FIG. 26.—*Tomb of Pope John XXIII. By Donatello and Michelozzo. 1425–1427.*
Florence Baptistery

FIG. 27.—*Tomb of Cardinal Brancacci. By Donatello and Michelozzo. 1427.*
Naples, S. Angelo a Nilo

FIG. 29.—Donatello: Sepulchral plate of Bishop Giovanni Pecci. Bronze. 1426. Siena, Cathedral

FIG. 30.—Donatello: Sepulchral plate of Archdeacon Giovanni Crivelli. Marble. 1432. Rome, Church of Ara Coeli

FIG. 31.—Jacopo della Quercia: Sepulchral plate of the Wife of Federigo Trenta. Marble. 1416. Lucca, San Frediano

FIG. 32.—Donatello and Simone Ghini: Sepulchral plate of Pope Martin V. Bronze. 1433. Rome, S. Giovanni in Laterano

putti and the side-faces (16 in. high) should be ascribed to Ghini (cf. Schubring, p. 196 ; Kauffmann, p. 91).—In 1427 Donatello and Michelozzo were jointly commissioned to execute the *Tomb of Aragazzi* in Montepulciano, but Michelozzo did practically all the work.— Two sarcophagi in the church of San Lorenzo (Figs. 33 and 34) came from Donatello's workshop.

FIG. 33.—Sarcophagus of Niccolò de' Medici. Marble. Florence, S. Lorenzo

FIG. 33A.—Sarcophagus of Giovanni de' Medici. Marble. Florence, San Lorenzo

The negotiations for the execution of THE SIENA FONT were begun with Jacopo della Quercia as early as 1415. In 1419 he made the model for the relief of Zachariah in the Temple, but it was not cast until 1430. He also contributed the five prophetic reliefs (P. Bacci, *I. della Quercia*, Siena, 1929). Ghiberti contributed two reliefs (1424–1427): Baptism of Jesus, and Arrest of John the Baptist. Goro di Neroccio supplied one of the figures of the Virtues ; Giovanni Turini played a considerable part in supplying two bronze reliefs, three Virtues, and three Putti. Donatello was commissioned to execute the remainder of the bronze relief, also the last two

FIG. 34.—Jacopo della Quercia, Ghiberti and Donatello : Baptismal Font of Siena. Marble and Bronze. 1417–1429

Virtues and three Putti.—This relief shows a scene from the story of John the Baptist, the DANCE OF SALOME 35–36

FIG. 41.—*P. Lorenzetti : The Dance of Salome. About 1325.
Siena, S. Maria dei Servi*

(20 in. by 22½ in.). Donatello's originality is admirably disclosed by a comparison with treatment of the same theme by an earlier Sienese painter (Fig. 41).—The two Virtues, FAITH AND HOPE or FIDES AND SPES (22 in. high), were finished in 1428.—Of the PUTTI (14 in. high), two of the finest are in their original situations on the font (Figs. 35 and 37), while another has found its way to the Berlin Museum (Fig. 36). According to Kauffmann (note 136), a fourth PUTTO, IN THE BARGELLO, did not

FIGS. 35–37.—*Donatello : Three Putti from the Baptismal Font of Siena. Bronze.
1428. Siena and Berlin*

come from the Siena font. Jenö Lanyi ascribes it to an unknown Sienese master ("Burlington Mag.", LXXV, 1939, pp. 142 and foll.). A putto by Giovanni delle Bombarde (a Croat bronze-founder who worked in Siena from about 1470 onward), surmounting a ciborium in the Fontegiusta church (Fontebrande) at Siena, strongly reminds us, in its style and movement, of this same cherub. (See a small reproduction in Lehnert's *Geschichte des Kunstgewerbes*, vol. I, p. 484). In this connexion may be mentioned other bronze putti executed by Donatello or coming from his studio. In London there is a CUPID WITH A FISH (Fig. 38, 1 ft. 3 in. high) ;

and another Cupid with outstretched arms ; a better specimen in the Bargello, and in the Estense Collection ; an angel with a torch in Berlin, and a putto with a torch in Leningrad. The CUPID'S HEAD in the Widener collection (Fig. 39 ; date from 1430–1435), at one time

FIGS. 38–40.—*Workshop of Donatello : Putti. Bronze.*
38.—*Cupid with a fish, for a fountain. London, Victoria and Albert Museum.*
39.—*Cupid. Philadelphia, Elkins Park, Pa., U.S.A., Coll. Joseph E. Widener.*
40.—*Putto as a candle-holder. Paris, Musée Jacquemart-André.*

belonging to the Duke of Westminster, is regarded by Schubring as an authentic work of Donatello (II, pp. 48–49, but see also K.d.K., p. 202 ; and W. Valentiner in the "Art News" under date April 14, 1928). Of this bronze the Louvre has a copy dating from the eighteenth century, perhaps by Houdon.—The TWO ANGELS WITH TORCHES in the Jacquemart-André Museum (Fig. 40) were, according to Schubring (p. 196), originally intended for Donatello's pulpit, and therefore date from about 1440 ; for other views of them, *see* Hadeln (*Rep. f. Kunstwissensch.*, 1909, pp. 382 and foll.) and Kauffmann, who considers them to have been designed for the high altar at Padua, which would make them date from about 1450. These two angels with torches, elaborately adorned with wreaths, are akin neither to the putti of the Siena font (1428), nor to the putti of the church of Santa Croce (about 1438), nor to the instrument-playing angels of Padua (about 1448), and it seems questionable whether they can have been the work of Donatello. The finest of all the bronze putti which are undoubtedly Donatello's is the *Amorino* or AMOR-ATYS, in the Bargello. The name "Atys" (or "Attis") implies a comparison with classical statues (*cf.* Figs. 42 and 43 ; also Osvald Sirén, *Essentials in Art*, London, 1920, pp. 103 and foll.). The winged feet and serpents twining between them remind us of a young Hermes ; but with this the little faun-like goat's tail of the "Amorino" seems incompatible (*cf.* Pl. 42). In the year 1778 the statue was transferred from the Doni House to the Florentine Museum, and it was first mentioned in the catalogue of 1782. The entry begins with a quotation from Vasari : "In the house of Giovanni Battista, the son of Agnolo Doni, a Florentine gentleman, is a bronze statue of Mercury by the hand of Donato (2 ft. 10 in. high), clad in a strange way ; the which is truly beautiful and not less rare than the other things which

FIGS. 42-43.—*Atys (Attis). Antique Statues.* (42) *Paris, Louvre.* (43) *Florence, Uffizi*

adorn his beautiful house ". The catalogue continues : " Vasari believed it to be a Mercury because there are wings shaped like ears projecting above each sandal, the footgear seen in some classical statues. But, for the rest, from the wings on the back of the putto, and from the way in which the hair is dressed, and also from the outstretched arms, we incline to think, rather, of a Cupid, as seen by an artist's fancy—after the matter of Giotto in Assisi, Gaddi in Florence, Lorenzetti in Siena, who contemplate the passions in their own way, resembling that of Dante in many respects, rather than that of the Greeks and the Latins. As to the clothing of the Cupid, it should be styled 'indecorous' rather than 'strange'. The poppy-heads which decorate the broad belt are, if we are not mistaken, symbolic of sleep, and the serpents entangling the feet must also be symbolic ". (*La Real Galleria di Firenze*, Florence, 1782, pp. 52 and 53.)— Only one passage from a classical author can be cited to explain this remarkable sculpture. It is to be found at the close of the tenth book of the *Golden Ass*, by Apuleius. Here is to be read the description of a play about " The Judgment of Paris ". We read (*inter alia*) : " There was a timber mountain to represent the famous mount of Ida which Homer sang of. It was a lofty structure of carpentry, planted with shrubs and trees in leaf, and from its topmost peak the workman's hand had made a fount to flow and distil its moving waters. There were a few young she-goats browsing on the herbage, and a young man in a beautiful tunic to represent Paris as the Phrygian shepherd, with a barbaric cloak depending from his shoulders and his head covered with a gold tiara : he was acting his part as the shepherd of the flock. A beautiful boy appears, quite naked save for the mantle worn by youths which covered his left shoulder, his fair locks falling brightly on either side, and among his tresses appeared two little golden wings which rose together in kindred form : his caduceus and wand

declared him to be Mercury. He ran dancing forward with an apple, gleaming with gold-leaf, in his right hand, and presented to the performer who personated Paris." I assume that Donatello's Mercury must originally have held a golden apple. The arms are welded on to the statue, and no longer represent the gestures they must once have indicated. (Kauffmann, note 170, tells us that these arms were a baroque supplement.) Donatello transferred to his Mercury the Phrygian dress which, according to Apuleius, was worn by the actor who played Paris, and Mercury thus resembled the Phrygian Attis. The open fly of the trousers discloses only that which the hermæ are wont to show. The goat's tail is well suited to the pastoral scene : to Paris, the goatherd, Mercury presents himself as a figure more or less like that of Pan. The snakes on which the boy is treading are those which usually surround Mercury's staff ; but I should not venture to assert that they may also symbolise the quarrel that ensued as soon as Paris had allotted the apple. We need not be surprised that the Mercury bringing the apple to Paris is so very like a Cupid, for we are concerned with the introductory scene to the story of Paris and Helen, the most notable love-romance of classical antiquity.—The fountain mentioned by Apuleius reminds us that Donatello's Attis may have served to crown a fountain, and this view is supported by a comparison to the " Cupid with a Fish " and to the " Bronze David."— I think the most appropriate way of describing this sculpture would be : " The Boy Mercury in Phrygian breeches, bringing the Golden Apple to Paris ".

Three popular statues which, between 1425 and 1431, Donatello contributed to the adornment of his native city, perished during the eighteenth century. I refer to the two Colossi and the Dovizia. Concerning the Colossi, Lord Balcarres wrote (Donatello, p. 34) : " Two other statues by Donatello have perished. These are Colossi (they were standing as late as 1768 ; Baldinucci, p. 79) ordered probably between 1420 and 1425, and made of brick covered with stucco or some other kind of plaster. They stood outside the church, on the buttress pillars between the apsidal chapels. One of them was on the north side, as an early description (*Memoriale*, 1510) mentions the Gigante sopra la Anuntiata, that is above the Annunciation on the Mandorla door. The perishable material of these statues was selected, no doubt, owing to the difficulty and expense of securing huge monoliths of marble. In this case one must regret their loss, as the distance from which they would be seen would amply justify their heroic dimensions ". The third of the vanished statues, THE DOVIZIA, the symbol of wealth, stood on the top of a tall pillar in the Old Market of Florence. Some pictorial and sculptural representations of them have come down to us. These free copies are usually ascribed to the Robbia, or the Santi Buglioni workshop. Specimens are to be seen in the Casa Buonarotti at Florence, in the Minneapolis Museum, at Berlin, and elsewhere. Donatello's Dovizia pillar is figured in a Florentine woodcut of about 1450, which has been described by Brockhaus (*Mitteil. d. Kunsthist. Instituts v. Florenz*, 1908–11, pp. 71 and foll.) ; in another fifteenth century Florentine woodcut, in the Berlin Print-room (Schubring, p. xxvi and facsimile of the Berliner Reichsdruckerei, no. 643) ; but the best and clearest reproduction is that to be seen in a painting (probably by a

FIGS. 45–46.—*Attributed to Donatello : Two Bronze Busts. Florence, Bargello*

FIG. 44.—*Giovanni Stradano : The Mercato Vecchio in Florence, with Donatello's Dovizia.
About 1570. Florence, Palazzo Vecchio*

Dutchman who worked at about 1600), with an artdealer at Paris (Kauffmann, Plate 7). Somewhat differently is the Dovizia depicted in Stradano's painting in the Palazzo Vecchio (Fig. 44). Cinelli's description conveys a good idea of the Dovizia (*Bellezze della città di Firenze*, 1592, p. 215) : " Its attitude is most charming. There is a basket filled with fruit upon the head ; one of the knees of the figure is bare, and so delicately modelled that it could not be improved ". (Cf. Carrocci, *Recordi del Vecchio Mercato*, text belonging to Plate 26). The Dovizia was carved of sandstone. On October 20, 1721, it was detached from the pillar in a weatherbeaten state, and was thereupon replaced by another.

During the ' thirties ' a few portraits were, on inadequate evidence, said to have been the work of Donatello. THE TWO BRONZE BUSTS IN THE BARGELLO (Figs. 45 and 46) were ascribed to him by W. Bode (*Amtliche Berichte*, LX, 1919, pp. 99 and foll.).—Schubring (p. 38) defends the

theory that the Sandstone Relief of a St. John (Fig. 47) were by the same sculptor. Differently composed, without cross and halo, treated in a purely portraitistic way and with more background, we find the same model on a relief in the Louvre (Fig. 47a). But the opinion that both these reliefs were sculptured by Desiderio da Settignano seems far more plausible. Still in dispute is the authorship of the painted terracotta bust of NICCOLÒ UZZANO (Fig. 48). Ultimately Kauffmann, after a careful examination, has come to a positive decision about this matter (pp. 47 and foll.). Franz Studniczka (*Vortrag beim Winckelmannfest*, December 6, 1911) has repudiated the idea that this bust was Donatello's work, and declared it to be a portrait of Cicero ; it has also been regarded as baroque and Spanish. Most misleading is the tinting with oilpaint, undertaken in the seventeenth century. It has been repeatedly maintained that the Uzzano bust must have been modelled after a death-mask (but consider Kauffmann's arguments to the contrary, p. 49) ; the assumption is supported by a comparison of the lineaments of the portrait with the shrinkage of a mummy's head (Figs. 49 and 50) ; we should also, in this connexion, examine the death-masks of Dante, Brunelleschi, and Lorenzo de' Medici which have been preserved in Florence.

After his mother's death, Donatello went to Rome, accompanied by his friend Brunelleschi. Concerning the

FIG. 47.—*St. John. Sandstone Relief.*
Florence, Bargello   FIG. 47a.—*Portrait of a Boy. Sandstone Relief.*
Paris, Louvre

FIG. 48.—*Niccolò Uzzano. Painted Terracotta. Florence, Bargello.*
(Ascribed to Donatello, and dated 1428–30.)

Filippo and Donato set to work and dug them out to find the foundations. From this a report spread in Rome, when they passed by, carelessly dressed, and they were called 'men of the treasure', for it was believed that they were studying necromancy in order to find treasure". How much influence these studies of ancient monuments had upon Donatello is shown, not by the works he produced in Rome, but by those effected after his return to Florence—the Cavalcanti Altar and the Choir Gallery, the Amor-

FIG. 51.—*Donatello : Tabernacle. Marble. 1433. Rome, St. Peter's.*
(The Marble Relief, Madonna and Angels, in the Lanz Collection, Amsterdam.)

journey Vasari writes (Hind's translation, Everyman edition, vol. I, pp. 274–275) : " Filippo and Donato met, and determined to leave Florence and go to Rome for a year or so, the one to study architecture and the other (antique) sculpture . . . At the sight of the grandeur of the buildings and the perfection of the churches, Filippo was lost in wonder, so that he looked like one demented. He set to work to measure the cornices and take the plans of these buildings. He and Donato were constantly going about, and spared neither time nor money. They left no place unvisited, either in Rome or its neighbourhood, and took measurements of everything when they had the opportunity . . . If pieces of capitals, columns, cornices, and bases of buildings were found buried,

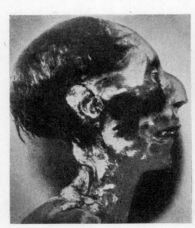

FIG. 49.—*Mummified Head of Rameses II.*
Cairo Museum

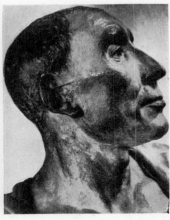

FIG. 50.—*Terracotta Bust of Niccolò*
Uzzano

Atys and the Bronze David. In Rome, over and above TWO TOMBSTONES (Figs. 30 and 32), he sculptured nothing but THE TABERNACLE OF THE SACRAMENT FOR THE OLD CHURCH OF ST. PETER (Fig. 51). It was made of marble (originally gilded), being four feet wide and seven feet high. In this tabernacle Donatello for the first time made a liberal use of putti, there being sixteen in all. The praying putti beside the door remind us of those of his teacher Ghiberti on the tabernacle in Santa Maria Nuova (Figs. 52 and 53), but are not so slender and delicately

74–78

FIGS. 52–53.—*Ghiberti: Angels, Detail from the Marble Tabernacle in Santa Maria Nuova, Florence*

FIG. 54.—*The Death of the Holy Virgin. 15th Century. Paris, Notre-Dame*

modelled, being sturdy, and somewhat short in the leg. The central portion consisted of a door in relief. This has disappeared, and has been replaced by a Madonna painting. We have no information as to whether the door was of bronze or of marble. A marble relief in the Lanz Collection (from the Casa Martelli in Florence) is supposed to have been a preliminary sketch for this tabernacle door.[13] In its measurements (2 ft. 5½ in. by 1 ft. 5 in.),

it is perfectly adapted to the vacant space. The combined photograph used for Fig. 51 shows the relief of the Lanz Collection as inserted into the Tabernacle. Very fine is the relief picturing the Entombment (on the upper part of the Tabernacle)—the first work to bear witness to Donatello's religious sentiment. Of interest is a comparison with similar French compositions of the same period (cf. Fig. 54). In connexion with the Entombment Relief on the Tabernacle we should also study two other reliefs sculptured somewhere about 1433. THE SALOME RELIEF AT LILLE is by Bode accurately dated "towards 1433"; Schubring assigns it to the Padua period, approximately 1450; in style it is unquestionably earlier than the Ascension of John in the Old Sacristy of San Lorenzo, which belongs to the epoch 1435–1440. Gonse believed that the Lille relief may have been almost contemporaneous with the Ascension at Naples (Plate 70), and must have been sculptured round about 1427; Kauffmann dates it at 1434. (Marble, 1 ft. 7 in. by

74

71

---

[13] Bode is opposed to this view. The same relief is in the Louvre as a bronze plaque, while there is a stucco reproduction (10 in. by 4¾ in.) in the Lanz Collection at Amsterdam; this little work has been ascribed to Bertoldo. (Cf. A. Pitt, *Quattrocento-Plastik der Sammlung Lanz*, "Münchener Jahrbuch d. bild. Kunst", 1912, I. Separate Reprint, pp. 13, 17, and 18.)

FIG. 55.—*Donatello: Christ in the Sepulchre, with Angels. Bronze. 1445-1448. Padua Sant' Antonio*

FIG. 56.—*Attributed to Donatello: Christ in the Sepulchre. Marble. London, Victoria and Albert Museum*

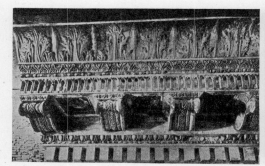

FIG. 57.—*Cornice of Temple of Concord. About 10 A.D., Time of Augustus. Rome, Forum Romanum (Tabularium)*

FIG. 58.—*Luca della Robbia : Cantoria. 1431–1438. Florence, Museo dell' Opera*

FIG. 59.—*Donatello : The Cantoria. 1433–1438. Florence, Museo dell' Opera*

FIG. 60.—*Dancing Putti. Relief on a Roman Sarcophagus. Rome, Palazzo Barberini*

FIG. 61.—*Detail from Fig 58*

73 2 ft. 3¾ in.) The marble relief, CHRIST GIVING THE KEYS TO ST. PETER, in London (1 ft. 4 in. by 3 ft. 9 in.) probably came from the collection of Lorenzo de' Medici. Kauffmann dates it at 1427; Schottmüller and Maclagan at 1433; Schubring at 1438. Kauffmann (p. 220) inclines to believe that this relief was originally designed for the socle of the Peter niche at Or San Michele. In this comparatively low relief (the so-called "stiacciato") with an impressionistically animated surface—especially in the background—Donatello came in sculpture closer than anywhere else to the pictorial style; the composition of the work reminds us of Masaccio. The relief showing CHRIST IN THE SEPULCHRE (marble, 2 ft. 7¾ in. by 3 ft. 9 in.) must belong to the same creative epoch, if Schottmüller, Schubring, and others are mistaken in disputing its ascription to Donatello. Pietàs showing half-length figures of the dead Jesus and his Mother were a favourite theme among the artists of Padua and Venice. That was why Schubring believed that the London relief (Fig. 56) must have come from Venice rather than Florence. In Rimini there is an early painting by Giovanni Bellini having similar composition. The relief we are considering was certainly later than the bronze sculpture of the same theme which exists in Padua (Fig. 55); it shows numerous advances, especially in the anatomy of the body of the Christ.

The Duomo of Florence, whose high altar was finished by Ghiberti in 1432 by the addition of the Zenobius sarcophagus, was designed to have two choir galleries

above the doors of the sacristy, one by Luca della Robbia (Fig. 58), the other by Donatello. THE CANTORIA, or choir gallery, contains upon the casement four-and-twenty marble putti dancing in front of a gold-mosaic surface, divided by ten pillars (Fig. 59). In the two circular areas between the middle brackets there were originally large bronze heads.[14] The choir gallery of San

79, 80

FIG. 62.—*Cantoria. (Ascribed to Donatello.) About 1460. Florence, San Lorenzo*

Lorenzo (Fig. 62), considered by Bode to have been Donatello's work, is ascribed by Schubring to an imitator of Donatello. The External PULPIT OF THE CATHEDRAL OF PRATO (Fig. 63) was designed for use on the occasion of a religious ceremony which took place

[14] Schubring (p. xxxiii): "We should represent the masks as having had the same character as that which Donatello gave to those on the socle of the bronze David. A similar mask is to be seen above Michelozzo's Baptist in the first hall of bronzes in the Bargello".—Cf. also Jenö Lányi ("Burlington Magazine", LXXV, October 1939, p. 147): "As to the cantoria of the Duomo of Florence, the right half of the main frieze is exclusively by Donatello's own hand; and so are the bronze heads which have hitherto been regarded as lost, but one of which we could identify".

built by Donatello with the aid of Michelozzo, was a series of dancing putti displayed on seven fields separated by twin pillars, and having a background of gold mosaic. According to Lanyi only two of the reliefs (the third and the fourth from the left) were by Donatello, and the bronze capital was "a masterpiece by Michelozzo". Still, this

Fig. 63.—Donatello : Pulpit at the outside of the Church. 1434–1438. Prato, Duomo

annually on March 25th. The cathedral claimed that it possessed, as an authentic relic, the Girdle of the Blessed Virgin. Once a year the bishop showed it to the populace which assembled in the square beneath the external pulpit. On the outer surface or casement of this pulpit,

Fig. 64.—Donatello and Michelozzo : The Bronze Capital of the Pilaster of the External
Pulpit. 1433. Prato, Duomo

Fig. 65.—Donatello : David from the Casa Martelli. Marble. 1434–1438.
Philadelphia, Elkins Park, Coll. Joseph E. Widener

bronze capital (Fig. 64), as Bode emphatically declares, is inconceivable without a detailed design from Donatello. The theme of David's victory over the giant Goliath was typically Florentine. Donatello figured it four times, twice in marble and twice in bronze (Plates 1 and 68, Figs. 65 and 66). The BRONZE STATUETTE OF DAVID in

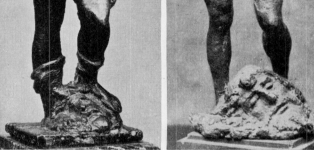

Fig. 66.—*Donatello : David. Bronze.* 1430–1434. *Berlin, Museum*

Fig. 67.—*Attributed to Donatello : David. Bronze. Paris, Louvre*

Cavalcanti in Santa Croce, for which he made an ornament in the grotesque manner, the base varied and twisted and the pediment a quarter circle, adding six infants[16] bearing festoons, who seem to be afraid of the height, and to be reassuring themselves by embracing each other. But he showed especial genius and art in the figure of the Virgin, who, affrighted at the sudden appearance of the angel, moves her person timidly and sweetly to a modest reverence, turning with a beautiful grace to the one who salutes her, so that her face displays the proper humility and gratitude due to the bestower of the unexpected gift. Besides this, Donato showed a

Berlin (Fig. 36 ; 1 ft. 2½ in. high) was a cast from a wax model. A remotely kindred statuette in Paris (Fig. 67), which Bode ascribed to Donatello, has of late been justly considered to have been the work of Antonio Pollaiuolo's school (L. Planiscig, *Piccoli bronzi*, Milan, 1930, p. 7). The MARBLE DAVID from the Casa Martelli (Fig. 65 ; 5 ft. 4¾ in. high) makes an unexpected impression by the over-ornate treatment of the hair, dress, and tree-trunk. It is somewhat akin to the MARCHING BAPTIST, now ascribed to Francesco da Sangallo.[15] (Cf. Kauffmann, *Sitzungsberichte d. Berliner Kunstgeschichtl. Gesellschaft*, October, 1931.) Vasari tells us that in the Martelli Palace there were several of Donatello's works in Bronze and marble. Of these the marble statue of JOHN THE BAPTIST (5 ft. 2¼ in. high) found its way to the Bargello. It was the last of Donatello's marble statues, for thenceforward he worked only in bronze or wood. One of the most beautiful carvings of the early Italian Renaissance, in its surface treatment it manifests an almost incredible perfection and refinement of technique.

Donatello's CAVALCANTI ALTAR IN SANTA CROCE (Fig. 68, 7 ft. 11 in. by 6 ft. 3 in.) was admired by Vasari (op. cit. vol. I, pp. 301–302) : "The work which made his name and brought him into notice was an Annunciation in macigno stone, placed at the altar and chapel of the

Fig. 68.—*Donatello : The Cavalcanti Altar. Sandstone. 1438–1440. Florence, Santa Croce.*

mastery in the arrangement of the folds of the drapery of the Madonna and of the angel, and by a study of the nude he endeavoured to discover the beauty of the ancients which had remained hidden for so many years ". How marked in this case has been the move away from the Gothic and a return to classical art is made plain by a

[15] Francesco da Sangallo, known as Il Margotta (1494–1576), witnessed the discovery of the Laocoon in Rome, in the year 1506. A sculptor of mediocre ability, he was for a time one of Donatello's imitators, as, for instance, in Peter and Paul on the tomb of Piero di Lorenzo de' Medici at Montecassiano (1532–1559). A signed bronze statuette by him in the quattrocento style, a John the Baptist, is in the Pierpont Morgan Collection in New York.

[16] These six putti are of terracotta, and not (as Schubring, p. 49, and our own Plates 81–82, erroneously indicate) of sandstone.

a   b   c   d

FIGS. 69–72.—*a and c : Heads of the " Three Graces," antique marble group, Siena, Libreria.—b and d : Details from the Calvalcanti Altar (cf. Pl. 83).*

comparison of the two heads of the Annunciation relief with the similar (but quite unnatural) antique heads (Figs. 69–72).

Donatello took a conspicuous part in the adornment of the OLD SACRISTY OF ST. LORENZO, built by Brunelleschi as the Medicis' Mortuary chapel. He contributed the eight clay-reliefs for the spandrels of the arches (Fig. 73); the two clay-reliefs above the doors (Figs. 74 and 75);

90–94

FIG. 73.—Donatello : *The Four Evangelists, and the life of St. John the Evangelist. About 1435. Florence, San Lorenzo*

and THE TWO BRONZE DOORS. (The individual areas are approximately one foot square. Plates 93 and 94 are enlarged to about twice the actual size). The extent to which in these laconic reliefs Donatello's work marked advances in expressiveness and nobility is manifested by comparing it with the representations by other masters (cf. Figs. 76 and 77).

FIGS. 74–75.—Donatello : *St. Laurence and St. Stephen ; St. Cosmus and St. Damianus. About 1440. Florence, San Lorenzo*

TWO BUSTS, ONE IN THE VICTORIA AND ALBERT MUSEUM AND THE OTHER IN THE BERLIN MUSEUM (Figs. 78 and 79), have been ascribed to Donatello, being brought into relation with the so-called St. Laurence bust of the Old Sacristy of San Lorenzo, and dated at about 1440. Kauffmann unhesitatingly regards the John in Berlin as the work of Desiderio da Settignano,[17] the St. Cecilia in London as that of an imitaton of Desiderio (Kauffmann, note 478). A. G. Meyer, Venturi, and Schottmüller were already disposed to doubt whether the Berlin bust was

FIG. 76.—*Two Prophets. Bamberg, Cathedral*   FIG. 77.—*Luca Signorelli : Two Apostles. Loreto, Basilica della Santa Casa*

the work of Donatello, but Colasanti (Pl. 112) was convinced that it must have been. The bust (of stucco, 1 ft. 6½ in. high) has been tinted in the baroque style, to accentuate the arching of the eyebrows and to make the mouth look smaller ; the cloak is of coarse linen, steeped in stucco. The over-ornate treatment of the hair conflicts with Donatello's style. The so-called St. Cecilia in London (terracotta 1 ft. 6 in.) has had its surface damaged by excessive scouring. Schottmüller has not expressly

---

[17] Desiderio da Settignano, Florentine sculptor, 1428–1464 ; famous for his portraits of women, stucco and marble busts, differentiated by their refinement of detail and by the romanticism of their conception from the monumental and naturalistic style of Donatello. Here is an interesting passage from Vasari (op. cit. Vol. II, pp. 33–4) : " In youth, Desiderio made the pedestal of Donato's David, which is in the duke's palace at Florence, introducing some fine harpies and vine tendrils all in bronze, very graceful and well-contrived ". On the ground of this statement, which presupposes a later execution of the bronze David, it has been assumed that this socle was subsequently utilised for Donatello's Judith. (Cf. G. de Nicola, *Rass. d'arte*, IV, 1917, p. 154).

repudiated this as a work by Donatello, but says it was "later than usually supposed". (*Bildwerke des Kaiser-Friedrich-Museums* 2nd ed. Berlin, 1933, vol. I, p. 9). But although what is spoken of as the ST. LAURENCE bust in

FIGS. 78–79.—*Attributed to Donatello (Manner of Desiderio da Settignano): St. Cecilia. London, Victoria and Albert Museum.—St. John. Berlin Museum*

Florence has been generally regarded as contemporaneous with the "St. Cecilia" it is now considered to be of later date. It used to have been assumed as having originated at about the same time as the bronze doors of the old sacristy of San Lorenzo, that is to say towards 1440, but it is now assigned to the post-Paduan period—round about 1457, or even later (W. Paatz, *Mitteilungen d. Florentinischen Instituts*, IV, 1933, p. 140). It is certain that the proper name of this late work of Donatello's is St. Leonard.

THE BRONZE DAVID IN THE BARGELLO (5 ft. 0½ in.) is likewise believed to have been of late execution. Kauffmann dates it after 1453 (pp. 159 and foll.) Vasari, on the other hand, held that the Bronze David must have originated before 1433, while Dvořák speaks of "towards 1430". Stylistically it is closely akin to the Amor-Atys, but technically it is not so advanced as the St. Francis at Padua or John the Baptist at Siena; it has much of the beauty and cheerfulness of the works of the sculptor's middle period, but is entirely lacking in the pathos and terror-inspiring qualities of his riper works. In my opinion the Bronze David must have been executed after Donatello had finished the Florentine choir gallery and the external pulpit of Prato, but certainly before he

FIG. 80.—*The eight Medallions in the courtyard of the Palazzo Medici-Riccardi in Florence. About 1457–1465. (Donatello's Workshop.)*

removed to Padua. Schubring maintained (p. xxxi) that the David must have surmounted a fountain, and he speaks of it as "the first bronze fountain of the Renaissance". The nudity of the figure is in conformity with the notion that it must have been cast to adorn the garden of one of the Medicean villas, and that the water must have spouted out of the apertures in the (now lost) columnar socle into a circular basin. Dvořák emphasised as follows the classical traits of the bronze David: "Not only the idealised head but also the body were modelled upon classical prototypes, the body recalling the Eros of Praxiteles (*Geschichte der ital. Kunst*, I, p. 83). Vasari insists upon the ultra-naturalism of the bronze (op. cit. vol. I, p. 305): "This figure is so natural and possesses such beauty that it seems incredible to artists that it was

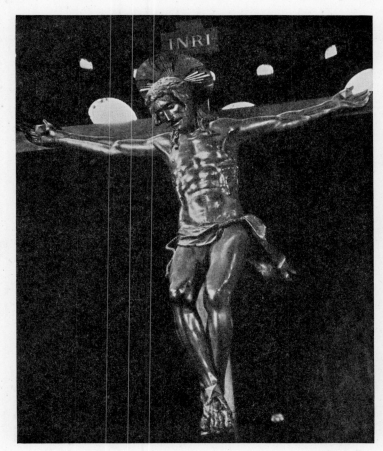

FIG. 81.—*Donatello: Crucifix. 1444. Padua, Sant' Antonio (Cf. plate 115).*

not moulded upon a living body". The court of the Medici Palace where the David originally stood was adorned by eight Marmortondi from Donatello's studio (Fig. 80). This ascription which, however, is contested, comes from Vasari (op. cit. vol. I, p. 306): "In the first court of the Casa Medici there are eight marble medallions containing representations of antique cameos, the reverse of medals, and some scenes very beautifully executed by Donatello". (Cf. E. Kris, *Meister und Meisterwerke d. Steinschneidekunst*, Vienna, 1929, pp. 17 and foll.)

In 1443 Donatello was invited to Padua, where he remained at work for more than ten years. There had long been close relations between Florence and Padua.

FIGS. 82–83.—*Donatello's High Altar, Padua, Sant' Antonio. Front and back view*

In Padua, Giotto painted the most notable of his fresco cycles; Petrarch stayed there for a time; and there Lorenzo de' Medici spent two years in exile. It seems probable that the summoning of Donatello to Padua was occasioned by the plans for refurbishing the Santo, the church of St. Anthony. For the roodloft[18] Donatello designed a bronze CRUCIFIX (Fig. 81). To begin with, the Christ figure was completely nude, the apron having been a baroque addition (Kauffmann, note 387). At that time (when the crucifix was first made) Donatello already had an assistant, a certain " Maestro Zuan, da Firenze ", whom Schubring identifies with Giovanni da Pisa[19] and believes to have collaborated in this work (p. 199 and note to p. 97.). The commission for the high altar of the church of St. Anthony, at Padua was not given till

April 13, 1446, but there must have been preliminary work of an earlier date, for the first casting was completed as early as 1447. The bronze altar was to be ready for the festival of St. Anthony on June 13, 1450. There was an enormous amount of work to do: seven full-length figures of almost life size, twenty-one bronze reliefs, and several stone reliefs. The present condition of the altar (Figs. 81 and 83) has been modified from the original execution. The first reconstruction took place in 1582, and there was a baroque modification in the year 1651; the assemblage of the figures and reliefs and the final reconstruction took place in 1895. (C. Boito, *L'Altare di Donatello e le altre opere nella Basilica Antonina di Padova*, Milan, 1897. A. Gloria, *Donatello Fiorentino e sue opere mirabili nel tempio di S. Antonio in Padova*, Padua, 1895. P. L. Guidaldi, *Il Santo*, 1932, IV. pp. 239 and foll.—A study of the attempts at reconstruction, especially the one by Detlev von Hadeln in the " Jahrb. d. preuss. Kunstsamml ", 1909, pp. 35 and foll.; others by Schubring, pp. XLII and foll., and by Kauffmann, pp. 109 and foll.— Regarding fragments belonging to the high altar in the church of San Lorenzo at Padua, see also G. Fiocca,

---

[18] The roodloft was demolished in 1652. The crucifix now stands above Donatello's (restored) altar to the Blessed Virgin.

[19] Giovanni da Pisa's name has become well known because the relief on the altar in the church of the Eremitani has been ascribed to him (Fig. 84). The putti frieze on this altar is to be compared with those on the pulpits of San Lorenzo (Figs. 125, 129–131), Donatello's work, to which Giovanni da Pisa certainly contributed (Balcarres pp. 189–190) Schubring likewise ascribes to Giovanni the execution of the " John Relief " (Plate 96), also the putto with the drum and the putto with the violin (Fig. 95). (Cf. Schubring, pp. 103–104, p. 199, and note to p. 106; in addition Schubring's *Urbano da Cortona*, pp. 62 and foll.)

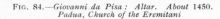

FIG. 84.—*Giovanni da Pisa: Altar. About 1450. Padua, Church of the Eremitani*   FIG. 85.—*Domenico Veneziano: Madonna and Saints. About 1450. Florence, Uffizi*   FIG. 86.—*Mantegna: Altar. About 1453. Verona, S. Zeno*

FIG. 87.—*Madonna on the Throne, with Angels and a Saint.*
13th Century. Paris, Notre-Dame

FIG. 88.—*Cimabue: Madonna on the Throne, with*
Angels and St. Francis. About 1300. Assisi,
S. Francesco

FIG. 89.—*Jacopo della Quercia: Altar, Madonna on the Throne and*
Saints. 1413–1422 Lucca, S. Frediano

" Burlington Magazine ", LX, 1932, pp. 198 and foll.)—
The attempts at reconstruction hitherto made have been
so contradictory that they cannot be considered here.
The general design of Donatello's altar can be deduced
from altars of the same date in which his influence was
conspicuous (Figs. 84 to 86) ; but in this connexion
earlier altars in Italy and elsewhere should also be carefully examined (Figs. 87 to 89). The figures of the
Paduan altar are somewhat under life size, the Madonna
being 5 ft. 4½ in. and the other bronze statues ranging
from 4 ft. 7 in. to 5 ft. Four accompanying figures
originally belonged to the Madonna (Fig. 90) ; two
others (Figs. 99 and 100) seem to have been added
subsequently. The Madonna is not represented sitting,
but in an attitude of movement, for she is rising from her
throne to show the Holy Infant to the faithful. This
Madonna is of an almost barbaric originality, but she has
her prototypes in the art of all times (cf. Figs. 91–94).
For his work upon the high altar of the church of
St. Anthony, Donatello employed more than twenty
assistants, among whom may be mentioned Giovanni da
Pisa, Urbano da Cortona, Antonio Chellino, Francesco
Valente, and during the latter part of his stay in Padua
Bartolomeo Bellano.[20] It cannot be proved that Niccolò

Baroncelli[21] worked in Padua as bronze-founder for
Donatello. It has been supposed that he may have helped
to cast the horse of the Gattamelata (Fig. 105) and also
that of Our Saviour in the church of St. Anthony (Fig.
81). Semrau ascribes to him the two bronze figures of
the high altar of the same church, St. Louis and St.
Prosdocimus (Figs. 99 and 100), which stylistically differ
much from the other five figures on the high altar—even
when we allow for the fact that the two episcopal staffs
and the pitcher of the Prosdocimus have been renewed.
The St. Louis is closely akin to the St. Maurice at Ferrara
(cf. Figs. 97 and 99), the Crucified of Ferrara to that of
Padua. It is of minor importance to what extent Niccolò
Baroncelli's son-in-law Domenico de Paris and his son
Giovanni Baroncelli collaborated in the bronze figures of
Ferrara, but it is significant that the commission for the
figures in Ferrara cathedral was first given to Donatello
(1450), since this provides justification for the view that
in connexion with some of his work Donatello may have
had recourse to Baroncelli and the latter's workshop.
THE BRONZE BUST OF LUDOVICO III GONZAGA Margrave
of Mantua, was believed by L. Courajod and A. Venturi
to have come from Niccolò Baroncelli's studio. There
are no less than four differing specimens of this bust.[22]
H. Kauffmann considers that the bust in the Jacquemart-André Museum (Fig. 101) is a copy, presumably
made by Giovanni Baroncelli ; copies probably, likewise,

[20] To Antonio Chellino Fabriczy ascribed (L'Arte ", vol. IX, 1907, No. 6)
the Madonna tondo in the Duomo of Siena, while Schubring attributes to him
the Matthew of the Evangelist Reliefs in Padua (Plate 95) and two of the putti
(Fig. 95). The " balance payable for an angel ", a sum which Chellino received
at Padua in 1448 may also relate to the Matthew Relief. Subsequently Chellino
went to Naples where (in 1458) he collaborated in the work on the triumphal
arch to Alfonso I at Castelnuovo (Fabriczy, " Jahrbuch d. preuss. Kunstsamml."
XX, pp. 12 and foll.)—Urbano da Cortona, 1426 ?–1504, worked at Padua
in 1446 and 1447. In September, 1447, he received payment for the execution
of a putto and for a symbol of one of the evangelists, that latter being presumably
the symbol of St. Mark (Plate 97). Since we agree with Schubring in ascribing
the execution of the symbol of John the Evangelist (Plate 96) to Giovanni da
Pisa, by parity of reasoning the execution of the symbol of St. Luke (Plate 98)
may be ascribed to Francisco Valente.—Bartolomeo Bellano (or Vellano) of
Padua (about 1434 to 1497) was Donatello's assistant from 1450 onward ; to
him Schubring ascribes the Sportello of the Paduan altar (Fig. 96). There can
be no doubt regarding Bellano's extensive collaboration in the pulpit of San
Lorenzo in Florence (Plates 141–149). To the same sculptor has been ascribed
the tomb of Narni senior, whereas the tomb of Narni junior may be ascribed
to the master who executed the Tomb of Santa Giustina (Victoria and Albert
Museum), and also the St. Jerome in the Desert (Widener Collection in Philadelphia ; reproduction by Schubring, p. 187).—Akin to this master would seem
to be Agostino da Duccio (1418 to about 1490) ; whom Schottmüller believes
to have worked in Padua towards 1445 (Bildwerke d. Kaiser Friedrich Mus. 1933,
p. 21), and to have been much influenced by Donatello, though he never worked
in the latter's workshop.

[21] Niccolò Baroncelli was, according to Vasari, a Florentine and a pupil of
Brunelleschi ; he worked at Ferrara from 1443 onward, and died in 1453. He
was also known as Niccolò da Cavallo because of the equestrian monuments he
made for members of the Este family. The first of these bronzes, commemorating
Niccolò III d'Este, was unveiled in 1451 ; the second commemorating Borso
d'Este, in 1454. In 1796 they were destroyed in a revolution, and therefore
cannot be compared with Donatello's Gattamelata. This is unfortunate, for
Baroncelli's Niccolò III d'Este was designed about 1444, some two years before
the Gattamelata. Among the pupils who studied under Baroncelli were, in
addition to his son Giovanni and his son-in-law Domenico de Paris, a pupil of
Brunelleschi's named Antonio Christoforo, who probably made the statue of
the horse-man, whereas Baroncelli sculptured only the horse. G. de Nicola
refuses to admit that Baroncelli was probably the executor of the bronze bust
of Ludovico III Gonzaga (Figs. 101–103 ; Thieme-Becker, Lexicon, 1908,
vol. II, pp. 517 and foll.) ; nor is there any evidence to warrant the not
improbable assumption that this bust was made by Antonic Christoforo.

[22] They vary in size no less than in other respects. The smaller of the two
Berlin busts is 10¾ in. high, the larger one (a cast from a wax model) 1 ft. 1½ in.
without the socle, and the Paris bust 1 ft. 2¼ in.

FIG. 90.—Donatello : High Altar, Padua, Sant' Antonio.   (Daniel, St. Francis, Madonna on the Throne, St. Antonius, St. Justina.)

are the St. Petersburg bust in the former Stroganoff Collection, and the smaller of the two Berlin busts (Fig. 102) ; the two latter being both distinguished by silver inlays and by very harsh outlines. But the head of the larger of the two Berlin busts (Fig. 103) must also be a copy, though much the best one. (Cf. Kauffmann,

p. 139 ; also F. Goldschmidt, *Die italien. Bronzestatuetten d. Kaiser Friedrich Museums*, vol. I, 3rd ed., Berlin, 1914 ; and the 4th edition of the same work, Berlin 1930, edited by W. Bode.)—During the summer of 1450 Donatello's stay at Padua was interrupted by a visit to Mantua, where he was engaged upon preliminary work for a shrine of

FIG. 91.—*Isis and the Infant Horus. Egyptian, about* 500 *B.C. London*

FIG. 92.—*Virgin and Child. French, about* 1250. *New York, Metropolitan Museum*

FIG. 93.—*Donatello : Virgin and Child. About* 1448. *Padua, Sant' Antonio*

FIG. 94.—*Mater Matuta. Etruscan. About* 400 *B.C. Florence, Museo Archeologico*

St. Anselm ; and to this year belongs the original of the Gonzaga portrait, which has been preserved in copies only.

In 1450 the high altar of the church of St. Anthony was finished. Exclusively the work of Donatello were beyond question the four bronze reliefs (1 ft. 6 in. by 4 ft. 2 in.) showing the miracles of St. Anthony (Plates 99–102). In the Miracle of the Speaking Babe St. Anthony is con-

99

Fig. 96.—*Workshop of Donatello (Bellano ?) : Sportello. Bronze. 1445–1450.*
Padua, Sant' Antonio

kicked his mother, and then remorsefully hacked off the offending foot, St. Anthony restored the lost limb ; in the Miracle of the Miser's Heart we are shown how, when the miser dies, a stone is found where his heart should have been, while the heart itself is discovered in the dead man's treasure-chest. Of the works in stone executed for the church of St. Anthony, the figure of a blessing God the Father has vanished " de sua cupola " ; gone likewise

102

Fig. 95.—*Donatello's Workshop : Angels, making Music. Gilded bronze. 1445–1450.*
Padua, Sant' Antonio

Figs. 97–98.—*Niccolò Baroncelli : St. Mauritius and Crucifixion. About 1453.*
Ferrara, Cathedral

ferring the power of speech upon a newborn infant, that it may testify to the innocence of its unjustly suspected mother ; the Miracle of the Mule discloses how one of the lower beasts recognised what human beings in their arrogant unbelief could not perceive (the bleeding of the Host) ; in the Miracle of the Healing of the Irascible Son, Donatello depicts how when a boy had lost his temper,

00

01

FIGS. 99–100.—*Workshop of Donatello : St. Louis and St. Prosdocimus. Bronze. Padua, Sant' Antonio*

is of grey stone (Pietra di Nanto), the background being of yellow-and-black mosaic; on the sarcophagus are three choice marble plates and green glazing.

As to other lost Paduan works by Donatello, Vasari reports[24] (op. cit. vol. I, p. 308): "For a nunnery he made a St. Sebastian of wood at the request of a chaplain, their friend and familiar, a Florentine. The chaplain brought him a rude old one which they had, asking Donato to make one like it, but though he endeavoured to imitate it, in order to please the chaplain and the nuns, he could not succeed, and though the model was rude, his own work was of his accustomed excellence and art. In conjunction with this he made many other figures of clay and stucco, and chiselled a very beautiful Madonna from the corner of a piece of old marble which the nuns had in their garden. An extraordinary number of his works may be met with all over Padua".

The Equestrian Statue known as "GATTAMELATA" (Fig. 105) was sculptured simultaneously with the high altar of the church of St. Anthony of Padua. Gattamelata signifies "spotted cat", a nickname given to Erasmo da

110–112   are two reliefs;[23] the only work that has been preserved is the Entombment of Christ, one of the most powerful and impressive of Donatello's compositions. The relief

[23] In his description of art treasures the anonymous Morellianus writes : "On the back of the altar, beneath the retable, are the dead Christ with the other figures forming a circle, and the two figures on the right with the two others on the left, in bas-relief, but in marble". One of the witnesses to the contract made by Donatello on July 23, 1443, for the work to be done at the church of St. Anthony was Francesco Squarcione—a man less notable for his own paintings (e.g., the intarsia-work in the sacristy of St. Anthony) than for his influence upon other artists. He possessed originals and casts of Greek and Roman masterpieces, which must have been known to Donatello.

[24] Vasari refers to additional lost works of Donatello's (op. cit. vol. I, p. 310) : "He also made in bronze the head of the wife of Cosimo de' Medici, which is preserved in the wardrobe of Duke Cosimo, where many other things of Donato's in bronze and marble are preserved, among others a Madonna and Child in marble, in shadow-relief, of matchless beauty, especially as it is surrounded with scenes in miniature by Fra Bernardo, which are admirable . . . In bronze, the duke has a most beautiful and wondrous crucifix by Donato's hand in his studio, which contains a number of rare antiquities and beautiful medals". The bronze bust of the wife of Cosimo de' Medici, the Countess of Bardi, has been erroneously identified (Cornelius, *Bildniskunst*, 1891, vol. II, p. 115) with that of St. Cecilia—though the latter is of stucco. The surrounding miniatures by Fra Bernardo (Fra Bartolomeo), depicting the Annunciation : Birth and Circumcision of Jesus, have, however, come down to us, and Kauffmann (p. 69) considers Donatello's Madonna relief in Boston, known as The Virgin in the Clouds, to be appertinent thereto. (Fig. 144). The bronze crucifix which Vasari saw in the studio of the Medici Palace has disappeared ; so has the cursorily described marble head which he claims to have seen in Urbino (op. cit. vol. I, p. 311) : "In the wardrobe of Guidobaldo, Duke of Urbino, there is a fine marble bust by the same hand, and it is supposed to have been given to the duke's ancestors by Giuliano de' Medici the Magnificent when he was staying at that court, then full of many noble lords".

FIGS. 101–103.—*After Donatello. Busts of Lodovico III Gonzaga, margrave of Mantua. Bronze. 1450. (FIG. 101 : Paris, Musée Jacquemart-André. FIG. 102, 103 : Berlin Kaiser Friedrich Museum.)*

FIG. 104.—*Roman bronze horses, from Constantinople. Since 1204 over the door of San Marco, in Venice*

FIG. 105.—*Donatello : the Monument of Gattamelata. Bronze. 1444–1450. Padua, in front of the Church Sant' Antonio*

Narni because of his watchful suppleness as a diplomatist. In his later years he was commander-in-chief of the Venetian military forces. He died at Padua on January 16, 1443. Immediately afterwards Donatello appears to have been commissioned to make the monument. In 1447 the socle, the face of which bears Donatello's full signature, was completed, and all the parts of the rider and of the horse were cast ; but the rest of the chiselling went on presumably till 1450 ; and disputes about money matters deferred the erection until September, 1453. The Gattamelata, the finest equestrian statue known to history, stands in front of the church of St. Anthony of Padua, to which the generalissimo, in fulfilment of a vow, gave his marshal's staff, and where he lies buried. (Height, minus the socle, 10 feet 6 inches.) The bronze head of a horse in the Naples Museum (Fig. 106), now commonly believed to be classical, was for a time considered to have been Donatello's work, and identical with the one which Lorenzo de' Medici sent to Naples as a present for Count Mataloni. Goethe saw this head where it had been

placed above a fountain (*Italienische Reise*, Mar. 7, 1787). A similar use had been made of a bronze head preserved in the Florentine Museum (Fig. 107), likewise regarded as classical, and originally used to crown a fountain in the Medici Palace. The Florentine head more closely resembles the horse's head in the Gattamelata equestrian statue. We may well suppose that Donatello was familiar with the fountain in the Medici Palace, and had learned something from it.

For the chapel of the Florentine congregation in the Frari church at Venice Donatello carved in 1450–1451 a wooden statue of JOHN THE BAPTIST (Fig. 109, 4 feet 6½ inches). H. von Tschudi (p. 30) contests the authenticity of this work. The original gilding and tinting have been retained, and the statue bears Donatello's signature upon the socle ; the inscription on the roll was added in the rococo period. (Fabriczy, " Jahrb. d. preuss. Kunstsamml.", vol. XXX, 1909, supplement, pp. 53 and foll.) According to Vasari, Donatello was simultaneously engaged upon carving a ST. JEROME for the Franciscan

FIG. 106.—*Bronze head of a horse. Hellenistic. Naples, Museo nazionale*

FIG. 107.—*Bronze head of a horse. From the Palazzo Medici-Riccardi. Florence, Museo archeologico*

FIG. 108.—*Head of a horse. Detail of the Gattamelata monument by Donatello*

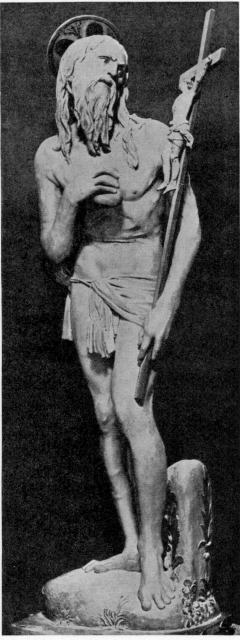

FIG. 109.—*Donatello: St. John the Baptist. Wood.*
1451. *Venice, S. Maria dei Frari*

FIG. 110.—*Ascribed to Donatello: St. Jerome. Wood.*
Faenza, Pinacoteca

THE BAPTIST in Siena (4 feet 8¾ inches). The John was cast in Florence in three portions, and was sent to Siena in 1457. In the documents for the same year relating to the Siena duomo we read that Urbana da Cortona had to deliver at Donatello's workshop in Florence a specified quantity of bronze for the " mezza figura " of a GOLIATH. I do not know whether this concerns a Bronze Head in Florence (Plate 136). Bode believes this head to have been executed by Donatello, but other authorities reject the contention. Its authenticity seems confirmed by a comparison with the earlier Rossore Head (Fig. 24), and also with the contemporary John (Plate 135). In 1457 Donatello was at work upon designs (probably in wax) for the BRONZE DOOR OF SIENA CATHEDRAL, but did not get beyond the drawings. In the Bargello at Florence there have been preserved three sketches of dubious origin, which Bode believes to have been designs for the never executed bronze doors to the sacristy of the duomo of Florence, but their style is so closely akin to that of the bronze pulpit of San Lorenzo that they may rather be related to the Sienese door (Plates 139 and 140, and Fig. 112). Certainly Donatello's was the terracotta draft for the so-styled FORZORI ALTAR (Fig. 111; 1 foot 9 inches by 1 foot 10½ inches, lacking the subsequent predella). Less confidence is inspired by a sketch

church in Faenza. There is now to be seen in the Faënza Pinakothek such a wooden statue (Fig. 110; 4 feet 5¾ inches) which Bode, Schottmüller, and recently Kauff-mann have identified with the before-mentioned St. Jerome alluded to by Vasari; but Fabriczy, Tschudi, Schubring, Bertaux, and Colasanti all refrain from mentioning it among the genuine Donatellos. The statue is in bad condition, having been much " restored " in 1845, and daubed over with paint; new are the tree-stump with the plants, the lower part of the socle, and the cross. The silk drapery round the loins is a tasteless addition which distracts the observer. When compared with these

128; 130–132

two dubious wood-carvings, the MARY MAGDALENE in the Florentine baptistry is extremely impressive. Here Donatello's later naturalistic phase is very forcibly disclosed, showing that ruthless glorification of the hideous which was first featured in the baroque style. Closely akin to this wood-carving is the bronze statue of JOHN

of the *Crucifixion* that has been preserved in the Berlin Museum (Colasanti, Fig. XLI), with feeble foreshortenings and displeasing intersections. The Forzori Altar, with perhaps also the three stucco designs in Florence, are the only sketches by Donatello which have come down to us; but there are no genuine drawings. (" Jahrb. d. preuss. Kunstsamml.", vol. L, 1929, pp. 9 and foll.) The Coronation of the Virgin, a stained-class window in the Duomo at Florence, was executed by Francesco di Domenico Livi in 1436 in accordance with Donatello's design that had been accepted in 1434. (Toesca, " Boll. d'arte ", XIV, 1920, pp. 3 and foll.) In the actual building, when one looks up at the quarterings of the drum of the cupula, it is almost as difficult to make out the picture as in the illustration. The predominant tints are white and blue (Fig. 113). A drawing, formerly in Vasari's possession, preserved in the National Museum at Stockholm may perhaps have some connection with

FIG. 111.—*Donatello : The Scourging and Crucifixion of Christ. Terracotta. About 1457. London, Victoria and Albert Museum*

FIG. 112.—*Attributed to Donatello : The bearing of the Cross. Stucco Florence, Museo nazionale*

the draughtmanship of Donatello (Fig. 115). It shows a putto holding garlands, as do some of the putti on the bronze capital of the external pulpit of the Prato cathedral (Fig. 114).

For one of the courtyards of the Medici Palace Donatello executed the JUDITH AND THE HOLOFERNES,[25] bronze group which was probably designed as counterpart to the bronze David. (Height 7 feet 10½ inches, including the socle ; 6 feet without it.) Schubring opines that the water must have run from the four corners of the mattress on which Holofernes sits, and from the masks on the socle.[26] The group is one of the most notable artistic features of Florence ; its boldness and fierceness have always had stimulating effects. A well-known criticism is that of Carl Justis : " A woman butcher about to hack off some meat for a customer ". Judith's attitude reminds us of that of the central figure in the relief at the Gate of Paradise in the Florentine baptistry (Fig. 116) but a lovely goddess of victory has been transformed into a terrifying sibyl, into a tragical creature, into a vengeful goddess of liberty. In Judith herself there is nothing typical either

of renaissance or of classical art ; she resembles, rather, the mournful Virgins of Gothic cathedrals (Plates 125 and 127). Unparalleled is the naturalism with which the body of the drunken Holofernes is displayed, this being seen especially in the swollen veins of the arms and of the twisted and impotent left hand. With this deadly earnestness of delineation, the observer should contrast the

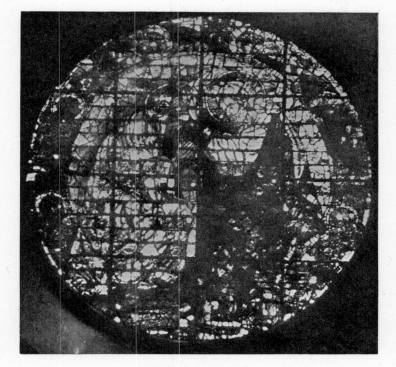

FIG. 113.—*Donatello : Coronation of the Blessed Virgin. Window-painting. 1434. Florence, Cathedral*

[25] From 1495 to 1504 the Judith and Holofernes group stood in front of the Palazzo Vecchio, the Town Hall of Florence. Then it was replaced by Michelangelo's David, and removed to the Loggia dei Lanzi. In 1916 it was brought back to its previous position in front of the Palazzo Vecchio.

[26] The reliefs on the triangular socle, which were partly hidden when the statue was *in situ*, were photographed when the group was being re-erected at the Palazzo Vecchio (Figs. 117–119). Comparison with a sarcophagus relief of pre-Christian days shows that here Donatello's work was influenced by classical examples (Fig. 120).

FIG. 114.—*Putto. Detail of the External Pulpit in Prato (cf. Fig. 64)*　　FIG. 115.—*Putto. Detail of a Quattrocento drawing (after Donatello?). Stockholm, National Museum*

FIG. 116.—*Lorenzo Ghiberti: Judith. Detail from the second bronze door of the Baptistery at Florence*

lively and animated scenes of the reliefs on the socle (Figs. 117–119)—the bacchantic sports of the putti amusing themselves at the vintage and celebrating their bacchanalia. These reliefs bear the imprint of a pupil's hand—probably the hand that executed the two dubious bronzes: the MARTELLI MIRROR (Fig. 122), of which several replicas exist, an allegory concerning the forces of nature; and the SWORD HILT in the Turin Museum (Fig. 121), which bears Donatello's signature (A. Bertoletti, *Arti minori alle corte di Mantova*, Milan, 1889, p. 99). From Donatello's workshop came two small bronze reliefs, one of which, the MARTYRDOM OF ST. SEBASTIAN

FIGS. 117–119.—*Donatello's Workshop: The three Reliefs of the socle of "Judith and Holofernes." Florence, Palazzo Vecchio*　　FIG. 120.—*Detail from the sarcophagus of Junius Bassus. Rome, Grotta Vaticani*

(Fig. 123, 9½ inches by 6½ inches), is in the Musée André in Paris, while the other, the CRUCIFIXION (Fig. 124, 1 foot 3¾ inches by 10⅝ inches)[27] will be found in the Camondo Collection at the Louvre. Schubring (p. 125) believes the former to have been Donatello's own work; Kauffmann (p. 256) takes the same view of the latter. As regards quality they are greatly excelled by two other bronze reliefs. The *Deploration of the Dead Jesus* ranks among six figure studies of almost incredible dramatic merit. We may suppose that this relief (1 foot 1 inch by 1 foot 4½ inches), since (like the Paduan Entombment of Christ, Plate 110) it has no background, was intended to be mounted on marble. The other relief, the CRUCIFIXION, comes from the Medici Palace in Florence. (Bronze, with gilt ornaments, 3 feet 0¾ inches by 2 feet 3½ inches) In the movemented liveliness of its composition it closely

137

138

resembles the Lorenzo "ambones". Venturi was disposed to ascribe it to Bertoldo, and he also believed that Bertoldo had a good deal to do with the work on the Lorenzo pulpits.

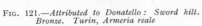

FIG. 121.—*Attributed to Donatello: Sword hilt. Bronze. Turin, Armeria reale*　　FIG. 122.—*Attributed to Donatello: The Martelli Mirror. Bronze. London, Victoria and Albert Museum*

[27] By mistake, in both editions, Schubring has depicted this relief "looking-glass fashion" (second edition, p. 174).

FIG. 123.—*Workshop of Donatello: The martyrdom of St. Sebastian. Bronze. About 1450. Paris, Musée Jacquemart-André*

FIG. 124.—*Workshop of Donatello : Crucifixion. Bronze. About 1450. Paris, Louvre (Camondo Coll.)*

149 These two *Pulpits in the Church of San Lorenzo at Florence* were the last work of Donatello. Pupils helped him ; among them Bellano and Bertoldo. Dvořák writes: " All, in them, that was Donatello's own work may be compared with the last work of such men as Titian, Michelangelo, or Rembrandt, for here has been assembled the experience of a long life, as if the octogenarian had been eager to record everything that stirred in his imagination". Parts of the pulpits were still unfinished when Donatello died, and the putting of all together and their erection did not take place until 1515. In 1558 and 1565 they were re-erected. About 1620 the pulpits were removed from the buttresses, and the gaps were filled in by wood-carvings.[28] The pulpit on the southern side of the nave bears Donatello's signature. The anterior side of the southern pulpit has three reliefs : the Descent into Limbo, the Resurrection, and the Assumption. The reliefs on the two lateral panels are the Descent of the Holy Ghost and the Watchers at the Tomb (Figs. 126 and 127). On the posterior side is a bronze relief, showing St. Laurence on the Grill. The two supplementary wooden reliefs represent St. Luke and the Mocking of

[28] These carvings are supposed to have come from the workshop of Pietro Tacca (1577–1640).

Jesus (Fig. 128). On the front of the northern pulpit are two reliefs ; the Crucifixion and the Descent from the Cross (Plates 141 and 142) : on the lateral panels are the Entombment of Christ ; Christ before Caiaphas and Christ before Pilate (Figs. 129 and 130) ; on the posterior side is a bronze relief showing Christ on the Mount of Olives, and two supplementary wooden reliefs that represent the Scourging of Jesus and John the Evangelist (Fig. 131).

A self-portrait of Donatello would appear to exist in the relief representing the Descent of the Holy Ghost. Peter, kneeling beside the Holy Virgin (Fig. 133), with T-square and other sculptors' tools beside him on the floor, has features that strongly recall those of Donatello as depicted in the woodcut given by Vasari in his biography (Fig. 134).

Four of the plaquettes are considered to have been Donatello's own work. (1) *The Scourging of Christ*, in bronze. Several replicas are known, including one in the Louvre, another in the Berlin Museum, and yet another in Strasburg (Fig. 135, $5\frac{1}{2}$ inches by $7\frac{3}{4}$ inches). (2) *Romping Cupids*, also a bronze (Fig. 136, $4\frac{7}{8}$ inches by $8\frac{3}{4}$ inches). A kindred panel, *Cupids frightened by a Mask* (Fig. 139), is usually ascribed to Bertoldo. Of this there are several

replicas : one in the Victoria and Albert Museum ; one in the Berlin Museum ; and one in Venice. (3) *The Virgin and Child* (Fig. 137, 4½ inches by 3¾ inches). Again there are various replicas : one of silver, in the Museum of Applied Arts, at Cologne ; two of bronze in the Victoria and Albert Museum ; and one of lead in the Berlin Museum (where there is also a large terracotta reproduction, Fig. 166). (4) *The Virgin and Child, in a niche* (Fig. 138, 3⅞ inches by 3¹⁄₁₆ inches). There are replicas in the Victoria and Albert Museum, in the British Museum, and in Berlin. It is questionable whether these four panels were really by Donatello ; and some of the others that have been ascribed to him were only the work of imitators (Figs. 140 and 142). Certainly from Donatello's workshop came a round plaquette showing the *Madonna and Child with Angels* (Fig. 143, 6¾ inches), of which there are two replicas : one, with the Capponi arms, in the Louvre ; the other, with the Pazzi arms, came from the Hainauer Collection in Berlin and is now at Philadelphia in the Joseph E. Widener Collection.[29]

[29] Cf. the relief (No. 1561) in the Berlin Museum, which has been ascribed to Bertoldo di Giovanni. The ornament in the background, the winged head of a putto with garlands, is accurately reproduced here.

Figs. 125-128.—*Donatello : The Bronze Pulpit on the southern side.* 1460-1466. *Florence, San Lorenzo.*—(125) *General view.*   (126-127) *The Reliefs on the sides.*   (128) *The Reliefs on the back*

FIGS. 129–131.—Donatello: *The Bronze Pulpit on the northern side.* 1460–1466. *Florence, San Lorenzo.*—(129–130) *The reliefs on the sides.* (131) *The Reliefs on the back*

In composition this plaquette recalls the lovely marble relief showing MADONNA IN THE CLOUDS (Fig. 144, 9½ inches by 1 foot 0½ inches) coming from the A. Quincey Shaw Collection, and now to be seen in the Boston Museum of Fine Arts. In treatment this relief resembles a stucco relief in the Berlin Museum (No. 2627), ascribed there to Desiderio da Settignano. Of this there are several replicas, one being in the Victoria and Albert Museum.

In the brief notices for which there is space in this catalogue no detailed account can be given of the almost endless number of MADONNA RELIEFS (Figs. 146—166) that have been ascribed to Donatello. Bode has carefully studied them in his *Florentiner Bildhauer der Renaissance*, but has probably been too liberal in his ascription of

works to Donatello. There really are no Madonna reliefs that can be accepted with perfect confidence as having been chiselled by Donatello. (Figs. 146 and 166.) Two especially fine pieces, both of them in painted terracotta, are the reliefs to be respectively seen in Paris and Berlin (Figs. 146 and 147). The Berlin *Pazzi Madonna* (Fig. 149), of which several replicas exist, has hitherto been unhesitatingly ascribed to Donatello. The so-called *Veronese Madonna* (Figs. 157 and 158), the most original of Donatello's Madonna compositions, would seem to have been preserved exclusively in copies.—Vasari maintains that Donatello was also engaged upon the restoration of classical statues for the Medici. He makes particular mention of a Marsyas, which is usually identified with a specimen in the Uffizi Gallery (Fig. 167).　　　L.G.

FIG. 132.—*Portrait of Donatello. Detail of a painting by Paolo Uccello (1397–1475). Paris, Louvre*

FIG. 133.—*Self-Portrait of Donatello (?). About 1460. Detail from the Bronze Pulpits in San Lorenzo, Florence*

FIG. 134.—*Portrait of Donatello. Woodcut, from Vasari's Lives of the Painters, Sculptors and Architects, 1568*

FIG. 135.—*Donatello: Scourging of Christ. Bronze. Paris, Louvre*

FIG. 136.—*Donatello: Playing Cupids. Bronze. Berlin, Museum*

FIGS. 137–138.—*Donatello: Madonna and Child. (137) Lead. Berlin, Museum. (138) Bronze. London. Victoria and Albert Museum*

FIG. 139.—*Workshop of Donatello: Cupids frightened at a Mask. Bronze. Florence Bargello*

FIGS. 140–142.—*Plaquettes by Imitators of Donatello. Bronze. (140) Paduan. Berlin, Museum. (141) French. Paris, Louvre. (142) Florentine. London, Wallace Collection*

FIG. 143.—*School of Donatello (Bertoldo di Giovanni ?) : Madonna with Angels. Bronze. Paris, Louvre*

FIG. 144.—*Donatello (?) : Madonna in the Clouds. Marble. Boston, Museum of Fine Arts*

FIG. 145.—*Workshop of Donatello : The Nativity.   Stucco.   About 1448.   London, Victoria and Albert Museum*

FIG. 146.—*Donatello : Madonna and Child.   Painted Terracotta.   Paris, Louvre*

FIG. 147.—*Donatello : Madonna and Child with Angels.   Terracotta, painted and gilded. Berlin Museum*

FIG. 148.—*After Donatello : Virgin and Child with Angels and Saints.   Painted Stucco. London, Victoria and Albert Museum*

FIGS. 149–166.—*Donatello and his School : Madonna Reliefs.*—(149) *Pazzi Madonna. Berlin.* (150) *Pazzi Madonna. Louvre.* (151) *Madonna with Angels. Amsterdam, Lanz Coll.* (152) *Desiderio da Settignano (?) Florence, Museo nazionale.* (153) *London, Victoria and Albert Museum.* (154) *Buggiano : Florence San Lorenzo, Old Sacristy.* (155) *Andrea Guardi : Berlin, Museum.* (156) *Madonna of the Via Pietra Piana at Florence.* (157 and 158) *Madonna of Verona. Berlin, Museum, and London, Victoria and Albert Museum.* (159) *Follower of Donatello : Lombardi Madonna. Florence, S. Croce.* (160–162) *Followers of Donatello : Madonna with five Angels. London, Victoria and Albert Museum, and Berlin, Museum.* (163–164) *Follower of Donatello : Madonna, adoring the Child. Paris, Louvre, and Berlin, Museum.* (165) *Follower of Donatello : Madonna of the Siena Cathedral.* (166) *After Donatello : Madonna of the Plaquette. Berlin, Museum*

FIG. 167.—*Marsyas. Hellenistic Marble Statue, restored by Donatello. Florence, Uffizi*

In the preceding catalogue, the monographs on Donatello are quoted under the names of their authors. "Schubring" means vol. ii of the series Klassiker der Kunst; *but the corrected edition of 1922, not the first edition of 1907. "Schubring II" means the chapter by the same author in the* Handbuch der Kunstwissenschaft, 1924. *"Dvořák" means the University lectures by Max Dvořák, 1918, which were printed at Munich in 1927.*

THE REPRODUCTIONS

Plates Nos. 70-73, 81-82, 137, and 139-142 are reproduced after
Museum photographs; all the others after photographs by
ILSE SCHNEIDER-LENGYEL

DONATELLO'S FOUR EPOCHS

I. *Juvenile Period,* before the journey to Rome, 1406-1432

(Cathedral Statues, and the Statues of Or San Michele ; Marzocco ; the wooden Crucifix ; mortuary Monuments ; Baptismal Font of Siena ; the two Statues of the Casa Martelli ; Portrait of Niccolò Uzzano.)

II. *Ripe Period,* 1433-1443

(Tabernacle of St. Peter ; Annunciation of S. Croce ; the last two Cathedral Statues ; the choir gallery of Florence ; the external pulpit of Prato ; the old sacristy of S. Lorenzo ; the bronze David.)

III. *Paduan Period,* 1443-1453

(The High Altar of S. Antonio ; the equestrian monument of Gattamelata.)

IV. *Late Period,* 1454-1466

(Judith and Holofernes ; Mary Magdalene ; John the Baptist of Siena ; the bronze pulpits of S. Lorenzo.)

1-2. DAVID. MARBLE. 1408-1409. FLORENCE, MUSEO NAZIONALE

3. LEFT HAND OF DAVID. DETAIL FROM PLATE 2

4. THE HEAD OF GOLIATH. DETAIL FROM PLATE 2

5. HEAD OF DAVID. DETAIL FROM PLATE 1

6. HEAD OF DAVID. DETAIL FROM PLATE 1

7. ST. MARK, THE EVANGELIST.
MARBLE. 1412. FLORENCE, OR SAN MICHELE

8. HEAD OF ST. MARK. DETAIL FROM PLATE 7

9. ST. JOHN, THE EVANGELIST. MARBLE. 1412–1415. FLORENCE, DUOMO

10.   HEAD OF ST. JOHN.   DETAIL FROM PLATE 9

11. HEAD OF ST. JOHN. DETAIL FROM PLATE 9

MARBLE. 1415-1416. FLORENCE, MUSEO NAZIONALE   BRONZE (COPY). FLORENCE, OR SAN MICHELE

15.   HEAD OF ST. GEORGE.   DETAIL FROM PLATE 13

16. HEAD OF THE MARZOCCO. DETAIL FROM PLATE 17

17. MARZOCCO
(THE EMBLEMATIC LION OF THE FLORENTINES). SANDSTONE. 1418. FLORENCE, MUSEO NAZIONALE

18. CRUCIFIX. WOOD. ABOUT 1418–1420. FLORENCE, SANTA CROCE

19. HEAD OF CHRIST. DETAIL FROM PLATE 18

20. RIGHT HAND OF CHRIST. DETAIL FROM PLATE 18

22. HEAD OF CHRIST. DETAIL FROM PLATE 18

23. HEAD OF THE SO-CALLED POGGIO BRACCIOLINI. DETAIL FROM PLATE 24

24-25. PROPHET. (THE SO-CALLED POGGIO BRACCIOLINI.) MARBLE 1419–1420. FLORENCE, DUOMO.
BY DONATELLO AND ROSSO

26–27. ST. JOHN, THE BAPTIST. MARBLE. 1420–1423. FLORENCE, CAMPANILE

29. HEAD OF ST. JOHN. DETAIL FROM PLATE 26

30. POPE JOHN XXIII. BRONZE. 1425–1427. DETAIL FROM THE COSCIA-TOMB. FLORENCE, BAPTISTERY.

31-32. ST. LOUIS. BRONZE. 1420-1423. FLORENCE, SANTA CROCE

33. ST. LOUIS. DETAIL FROM PLATE 31

34. BISHOP GIOVANNI PECCI. BRONZE. 1426.
DETAIL FROM THE SEPULCHRAL PLATE ON THE PECCI TOMB. SIENA, CATHEDRAL

35. THE DANCE OF SALOME. BRONZE RELIEF. 1425–1427. SIENA, CATHEDRAL FONT

36. SALOME-RELIEF. DETAIL FROM PLATE 35

39. PUTTO. BRONZE. 1429–1430. SIENA, CUPOLA OF THE CATHEDRAL FONT

40. PUTTO. BRONZE. ABOUT 1430. (WORKSHOP OR FOLLOWER OF DONATELLO). FLORENCE, MUSEO NAZIONALE

41. THE SO-CALLED AMOR-ATYS. BRONZE. 1430–1434. FLORENCE, MUSEO NAZIONALE

43. AMOR-ATYS. DETAIL FROM PLATE 41

44-45. JEREMIAH. MARBLE. 1427-1435. FLORENCE, CAMPANILE

46. JEREMIAH. DETAIL FROM PLATE 44

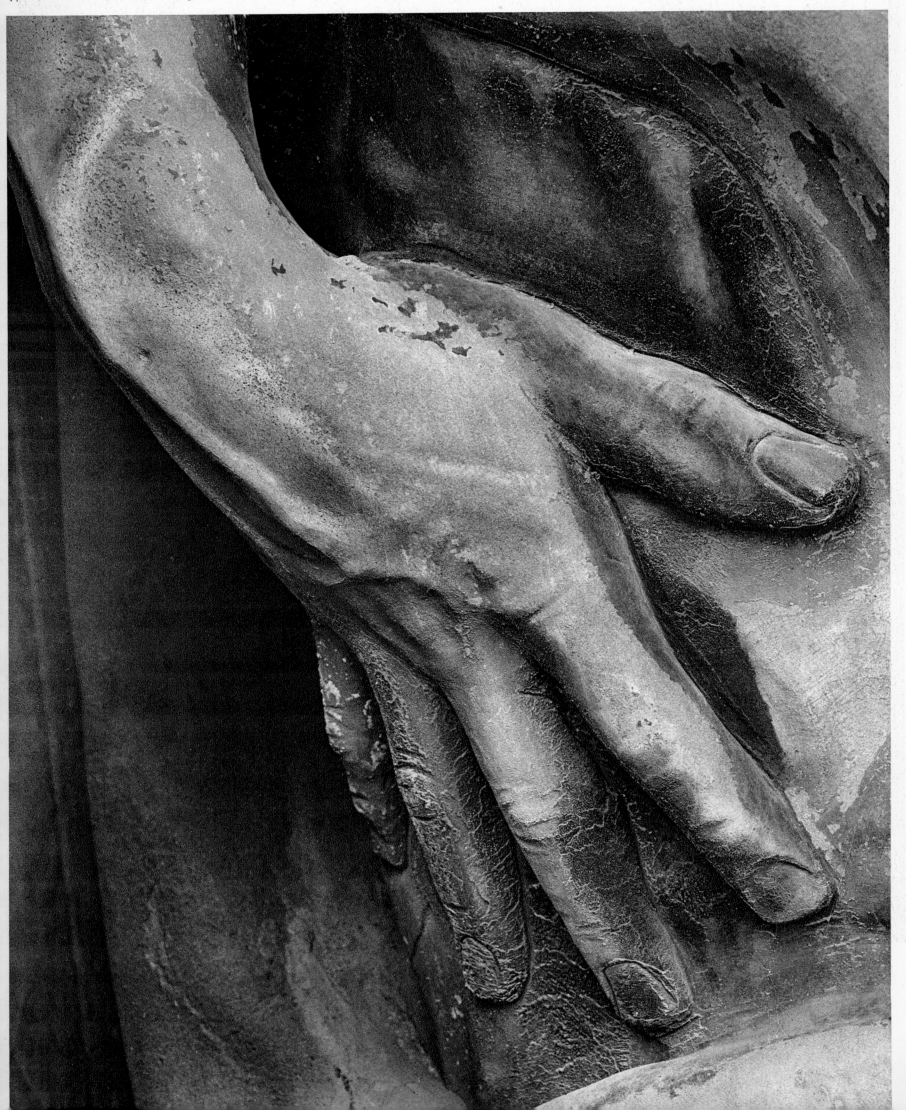

48. HEAD OF JEREMIAH. DETAIL FROM PLATE 44

49. THE SO-CALLED ZUCCONE (OR BALD-PATE).
MARBLE. 1435-1436. FLORENCE, CAMPANILE

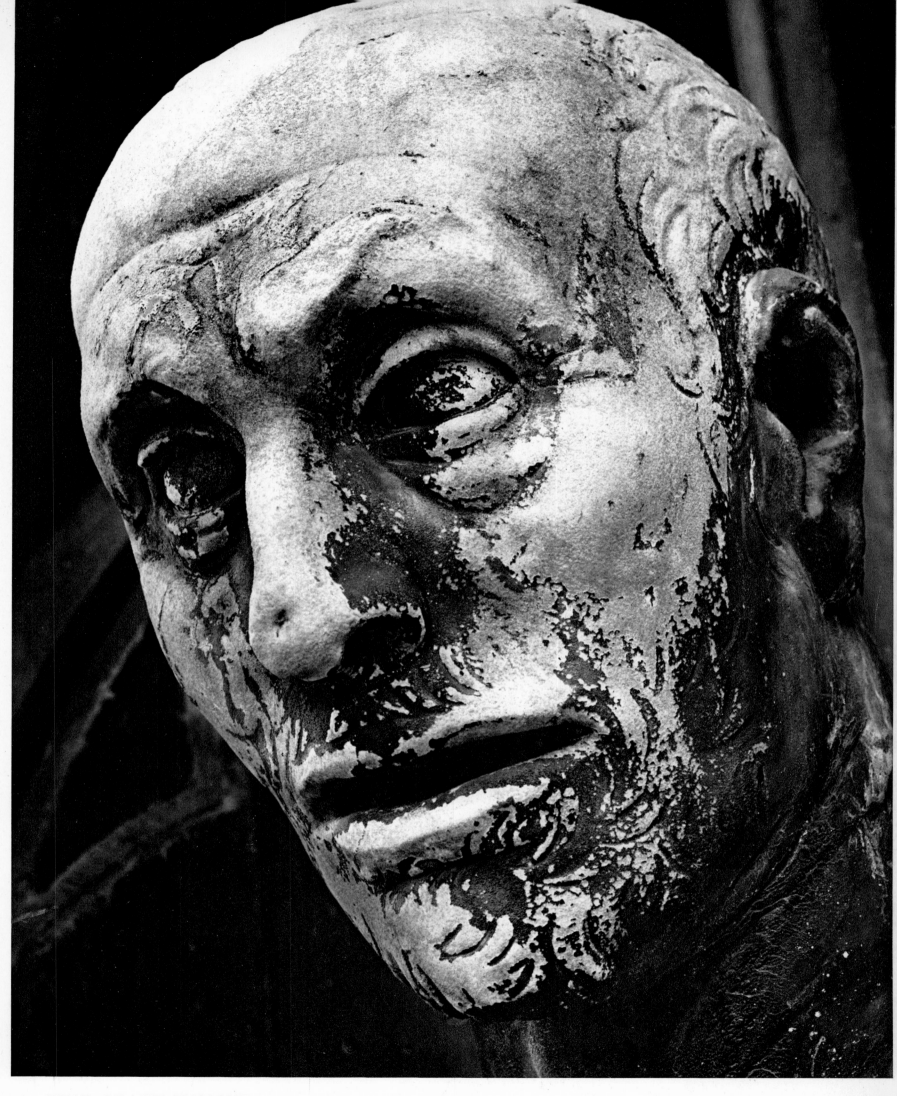

50. HEAD OF THE ZUCCONE. DETAIL FROM PLATE 49

51. RIGHT HAND OF THE ZUCCONE.   DETAIL FROM PLATE 49

52. LEFT HAND OF THE ZUCCONE. DETAIL FROM PLATE 49

53. PORTRAIT BUST OF NICCOLO DA UZZANO. PAINTED TERRACOTTA. ABOUT 1430. FLORENCE, MUSEO NAZIONALE

54. LEFT HAND OF ST. JOHN. DETAIL FROM PLATE 55

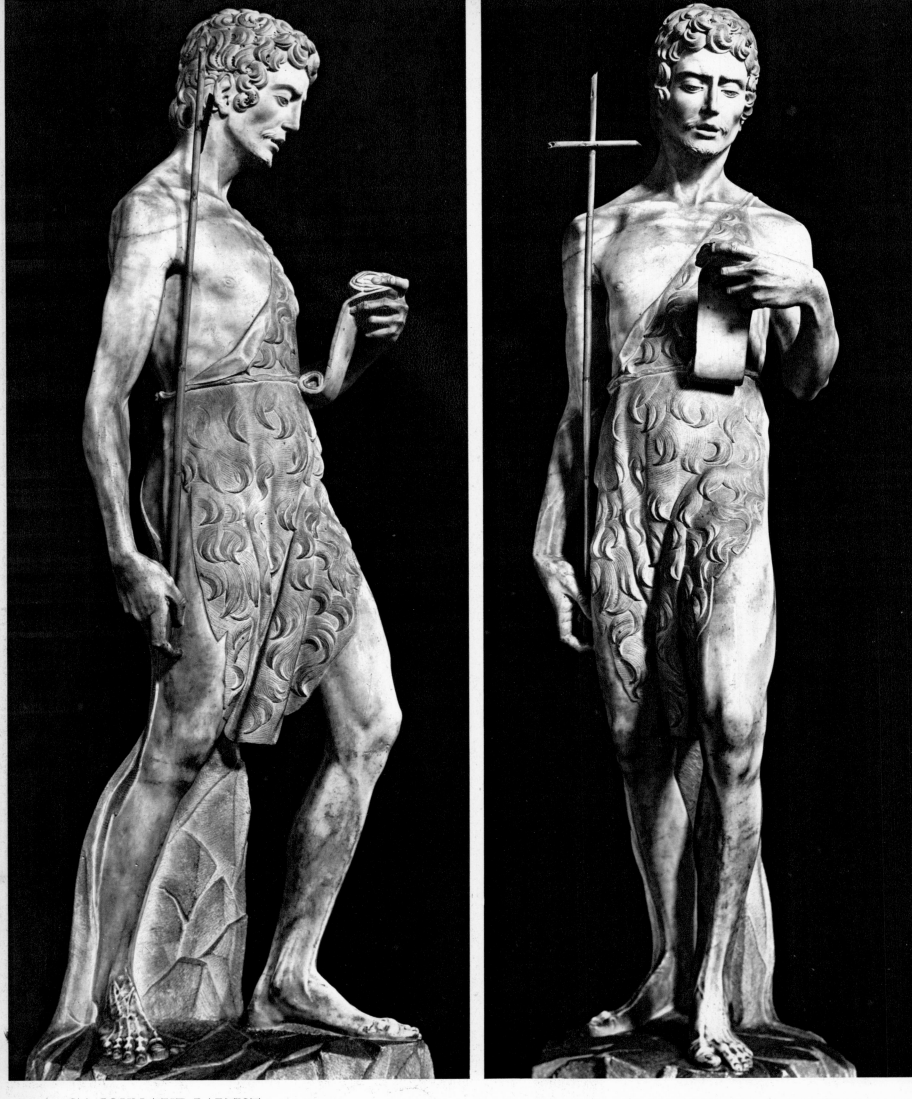

55-56. ST. JOHN THE BAPTIST.
(DONATELLO'S WORKSHOP OR BY FRANCESCO DA SANGALLO?). MARBLE. FLORENCE, MUSEO NAZIONALE

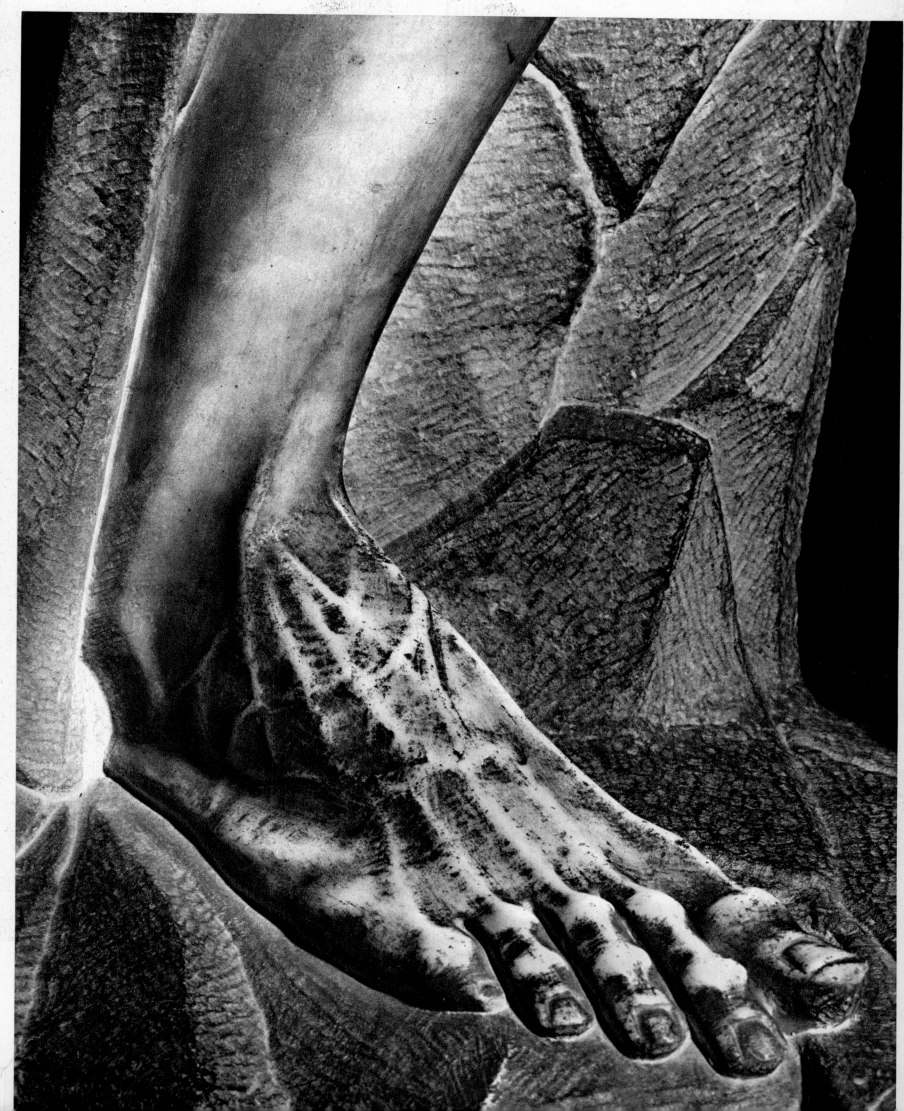

58. HEAD OF ST. JOHN. DETAIL FROM PLATE 56

59. HEAD OF ST. JOHN. DETAIL FROM PLATE 60

62. HEAD OF ST. JOHN. DETAIL FROM PLATE 61

63. RIGHT HAND OF ST. JOHN.   DETAIL FROM PLATE 60

64. LEFT HAND OF ST. JOHN. DETAIL FROM PLATE 60

65. POPE MARTIN V.   BRONZE RELIEF.   1433.
DETAIL FROM THE SEPULCHRAL PLATE ON HIS TOMB.   ROME, SAN GIOVANNI IN LATERANO

66. HEAD OF GOLIATH. DETAIL FROM PLATE 68

67. DAVID. BACK VIEW. DETAIL FROM PLATE 68

68-69. DAVID. BRONZE. 1438-1443. FLORENCE, MUSEO NAZIONALE

70. THE ASSUMPTION OF THE VIRGIN.
MARBLE RELIEF ON THE TOMB OF CARDINAL RINALDO BRANCACCI. 1427. NAPLES, SAN ANGELO A NILO

71. THE DANCE OF SALOME.   MARBLE RELIEF.   ABOUT 1433.   LILLE, MUSÉE WICAR

72-73. CHRIST GIVING THE KEYS TO ST. PETER.
MARBLE RELIEF (AND DETAIL). ABOUT 1433. LONDON, VICTORIA AND ALBERT MUSEUM

74-76. ENTOMBMENT OF CHRIST.
MARBLE RELIEF (AND TWO DETAILS). DETAIL OF A TABERNACLE. 1433. ROME, ST. PETER'S

77. ANGELS. MARBLE. 1433. DETAIL OF A TABERNACLE. ROME, ST. PETER'S

78. ANGELS. MARBLE. 1433. DETAIL FROM A TABERNACLE. ROME, ST. PETER'S

79. DANCING ANGELS. MARBLE. 1433–1438.
DETAIL OF THE CANTORIA, FORMERLY IN THE CATHEDRAL. FLORENCE, MUSEO DELL' OPERA DI S. MARIA DEL FIORE

80. DANCING ANGELS. MARBLE. 1433–1438.
DETAIL OF THE CANTORIA, FORMERLY IN THE CATHEDRAL. FLORENCE, MUSEO DELL' OPERA DI S. MARIA DEL FIORE

81–82. ANGELS. SANDSTONE. 1438–1440. DETAIL OF THE CALVALCANTI ALTAR. FLORENCE, SANTA CROCE

83. THE ANNUNCIATION.
BLUISH SANDSTONE, PARTLY GILDED. 1438–1440. RELIEF ON THE CALVALCANTI ALTAR. FLORENCE, SANTA CROCE

84. THE ANGEL OF THE ANNUNCIATION. DETAIL FROM PLATE 83

85.　THE HOLY VIRGIN.　DETAIL FROM PLATE 84

86. HEAD OF THE ANGEL. DETAIL FROM PLATE 83

87. HEAD OF THE VIRGIN. DETAIL FROM PLATE 83

88. ST. LEONARD.
(FORMERLY CALLED ST. LAURENCE.)   TERRACOTTA.   1447–1457 (?)   FLORENCE, SAN LORENZO, OLD SACRISTY

89. ST. LEONARD. DETAIL FROM PLATE 88

90-91. THE TWO BRONZE DOORS IN THE OLD SACRISTY. 1439-1443. FLORENCE, SAN LORENZO

92. TWO APOSTLES. DETAIL FROM PLATE 90

93. APOSTLE. DETAIL FROM PLATE 90

94. APOSTLE. DETAIL FROM PLATE 90

95. SYMBOL OF ST. MATTHEW, THE EVANGELIST. BRONZE. 1445–1448. PADUA, SANT' ANTONIO

96. SYMBOL OF ST. JOHN, THE EVANGELIST. BRONZE. 1445-1448. PADUA, SANT' ANTONIO

97. SYMBOL OF ST. MARK, THE EVANGELIST. BRONZE. 1445–1448. PADUA, SANT' ANTONIO

98. SYMBOL OF ST. LUKE, THE EVANGELIST. BRONZE. 1445–1448. PADUA, SANT' ANTONIO

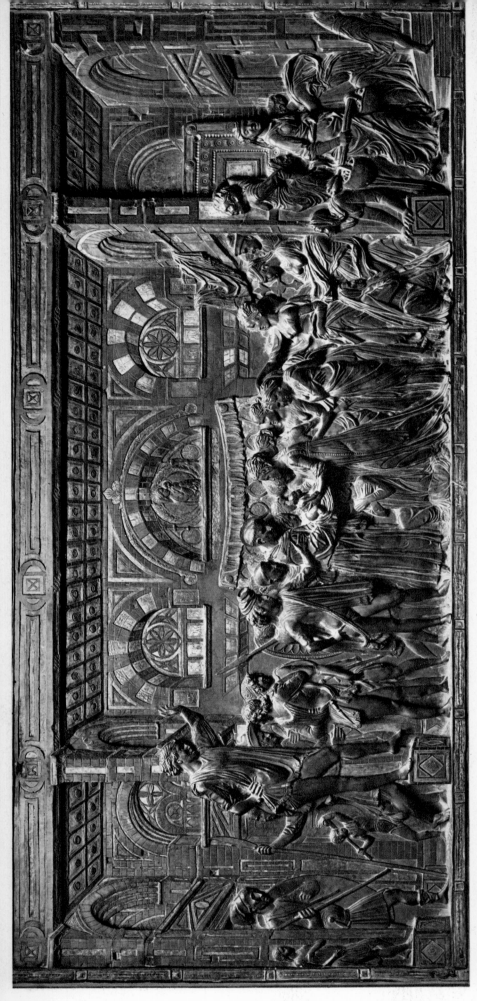

99-100. MIRACLE OF THE SPEAKING BABE—MIRACLE OF THE MULE. BRONZE. 1445-1448. PADUA, SANT' ANTONIO

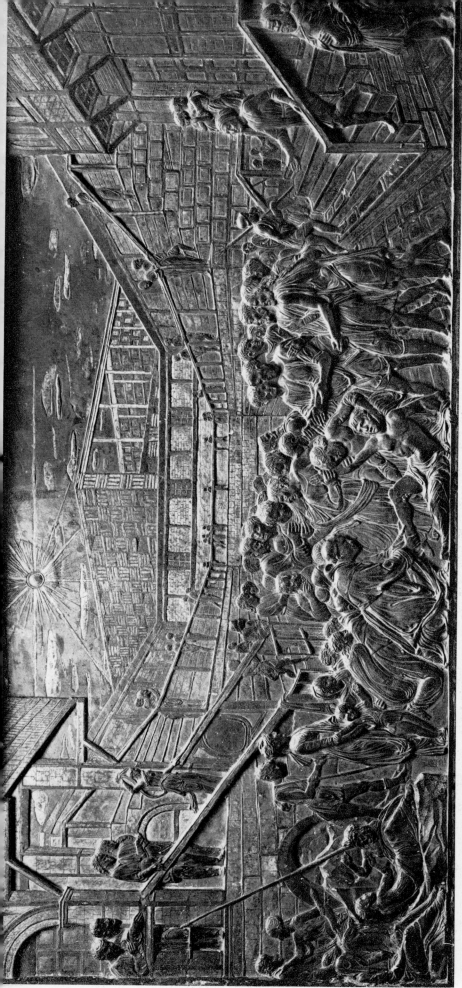

01–102. MIRACLE OF THE HEALING OF THE IRASCIBLE SON—MIRACLE OF THE MISER'S HEART.
BRONZE. 1445–1448. PADUA, SANT' ANTONIO

103. HEALING OF THE IRASCIBLE SON.   DETAIL FROM PLATE 101

105. MIRACLE OF THE SPEAKING BABE. DETAIL FROM PLATE 99

106. MIRACLE OF THE MISER'S HEART. DETAIL FROM PLATE 102

107. MIRACLE OF THE MULE. DETAIL FROM PLATE 100

108-109. MIRACLE OF THE MULE. DETAILS FROM PLATE 100

110. ENTOMBMENT OF CHRIST. STONE. 1445-1448. PADUA, SANT' ANTONIO

III. ENTOMBMENT OF CHRIST. DETAIL FROM PLATE 110

112. ENTOMBMENT OF CHRIST. DETAIL FROM PLATE 110

113. PIETÀ. BRONZE. 1445–1448. PADUA, SANT' ANTONIO

114. HEAD OF CHRIST. DETAIL FROM PLATE 113

115. CRUCIFIX. (DETAIL). BRONZE. 1444. PADUA, SANT' ANTONIO

119.   HEAD OF ST. FRANCIS.   DETAIL FROM PLATE 117

120. EQUESTRIAN MONUMENT OF GENERAL GATTAMELATA.
(DETAIL). BRONZE. 1444-1450. PADUA, IN FRONT OF THE CHURCH SANT' ANTONIO

121. HEAD OF GATTAMELATA. DETAIL FROM PLATE 120

122. HEAD OF GATTAMELATA. DETAIL FROM PLATE 120

123. HORSE HEAD. DETAIL OF THE EQUESTRIAN MONUMENT OF GATTAMELATA. BRONZE. 1444–1450. PADUA

124. JUDITH AND HOLOFERNES. BRONZE. 1455–1457. IN FRONT OF THE PALAZZO VECCHIO, FLORENCE

125. HEAD OF JUDITH. DETAIL FROM PLATE 124

26. HEAD OF HOLOFERNES. DETAIL FROM PLATE 124

127. HEAD OF JUDITH. DETAIL FROM PLATE 126

128. ST. MARY MAGDALEN.
WOOD. ABOUT 1455. FLORENCE, BAPTISTERY

129. ST. JOHN, THE EVANGELIST.
BRONZE. 1457. SIENA, CATHEDRAL

130. ST. MARY MAGDALEN. DETAIL FROM PLATE 128

131. THE HANDS OF ST. MARY MAGDALEN. DETAIL FROM PLATE 128

132. HEAD OF ST. MARY MAGDALEN. DETAIL FROM PLATE 128

134.   HEAD OF ST. JOHN.   DETAIL FROM PLATE 129

135. ST. JOHN. DETAIL FROM PLATE 129

136. DECORATIVE BRONZE HEAD. 1455-1457. FLORENCE, MUSEO NAZIONALE

137. PIETÀ. BRONZE RELIEF. ABOUT 1455-1457. LONDON, VICTORIA AND ALBERT MUSEUM

138. THE CRUCIFIXION. BRONZE. ABOUT 1455–1457. FLORENCE, MUSEO NAZIONALE

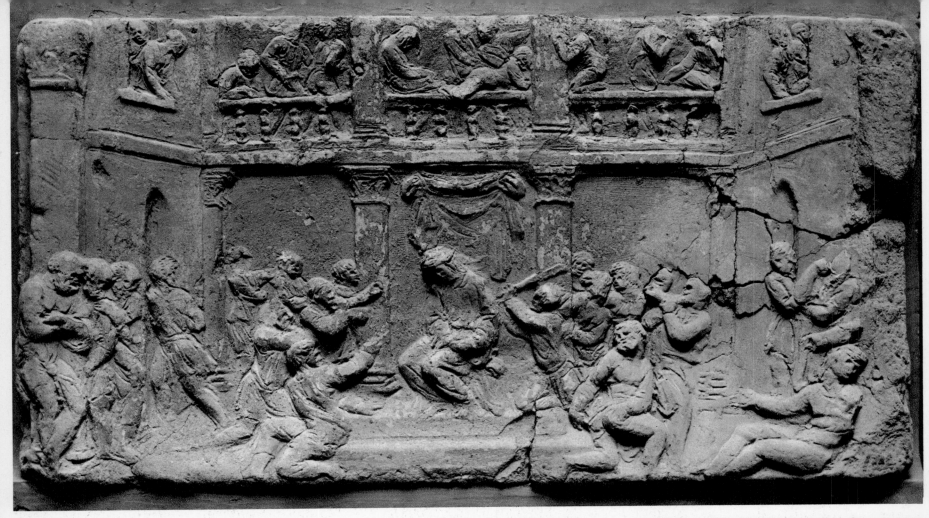

139-140. THE SCOURGING OF CHRIST—CHRIST BEFORE PILATUS. SKETCHES IN TERRACOTTA. (ATTRIBUTED TO
DONATELLO, AS MODELS FOR THE BRONZE DOOR OF THE DUOMO, 1437.) STUCCO. FLORENCE, MUSEO NAZIONALE

141–142. CRUCIFIXION—DEPOSITION FROM THE CROSS. 1460–1466. BRONZE RELIEFS OF THE PULPIT ON THE NORTHERN SIDE OF THE MIDDLE NAVE, SAN LORENZO, FLORENCE. (BY DONATELLO AND HIS SCHOOL.)

143. CHRIST, THE VIRGIN AND ST. MARY MAGDALEN. 1460–1466.
DETAIL FROM A BRONZE RELIEF ON THE SOUTHERN SIDE OF THE MIDDLE NAVE, SAN LORENZO, FLORENCE

144. ST. JOHN THE BAPTIST. 1460–1466.
DETAIL FROM A BRONZE RELIEF ON THE SOUTHERN SIDE OF THE MIDDLE NAVE, SAN LORENZO, FLORENCE

145. SAINTS. 1460–1466.
DETAIL FROM A BRONZE RELIEF ON THE SOUTHERN SIDE OF THE MIDDLE NAVE, SAN LORENZO, FLORENCE

146. SAINTS. 1460–1466. DETAIL FROM A BRONZE RELIEF OF THE PULPIT ON THE SOUTHERN SIDE OF THE MIDDLE NAVE, SAN LORENZO, FLORENCE

147. CHRIST RISING FROM HIS GRAVE. 1460–1466. DETAIL FROM A BRONZE RELIEF OF THE PULPIT ON THE
SOUTHERN SIDE OF THE MIDDLE NAVE, SAN LORENZO, FLORENCE

148. RESURRECTION OF CHRIST. 1460–1466. DETAIL FROM A BRONZE RELIEF OF THE PULPIT ON THE SOUTHERN SIDE OF THE MIDDLE NAVE, SAN LORENZO, FLORENCE

49. WOMEN WITH CHRISMATORY. 1460–1466. DETAIL FROM A BRONZE RELIEF OF THE PULPIT ON THE SOUTHERN SIDE OF THE MIDDLE NAVE, SAN LORENZO, FLORENCE

INDEX OF MUSEUMS

INDEX OF MUSEUMS, COLLECTIONS AND PLACES

AMSTERDAM, LANZ COLL.
Madonna Relief, fig. 151 (51).

BERLIN, KAISER FRIEDRICH MUSEUM.
Madonna, fig. 5.
John the Baptist, fig. 22.
Scourging of Christ, fig. 25.
Putto, fig. 36.
David, fig. 66.
John the Baptist, fig. 79.
Lodovico Gonzaga, figs. 102, 103.
Plaquettes, figs. 136, 137, 140.
Madonna Reliefs, figs. 147, 149, 157, 161, 162, 164, 166.

BOSTON, MUSEUM OF FINE ARTS.
Madonna in the Clouds, fig. 144.

BOSTON, QUINCEY SHAW COLL.
(Madonna in the Clouds, fig. 144).

FAENZA, PINACOTECA.
St. Jerome, fig. 110.

FLORENCE, BAPTISTERY.
Tomb of Pope John XXIII, fig. 26, 28 ; pl. 30.
Mary Magdalene, pl. 128, 130–132.

FLORENCE, DUOMO, PORTA MANDORLA.
Two Prophets, figs. 3–4.

FLORENCE, DUOMO, CAMPANILE.
So-called Poggio Bracciolini, pl. 23–25.
John the Baptist, pl. 26–29.
So-called Habbacuc, fig. 18.
So-called Moses, fig. 19.
Abraham and Isaac, fig. 20.
Jeremiah, pl. 44–48.
So-called Zuccone, pl. 49–52.

FLORENCE, DUOMO.
John, the Evangelist, pl. 9–11.
Coronation of the Virgin, fig. 113.
(David, pl. 1–6).

FLORENCE, MUSEO DELL' OPERA.
Cantoria, fig. 59 ; pl. 79–80.

FLORENCE, S. CROCE.
Crucifix, pl. 18–22.
The Cavalcanti Altar, fig. 68 ; pl. 81–87.
Lombardi Madonna, fig. 159.

FLORENCE, S. LORENZO.
Cantoria, fig. 62.
The Evangelist Reliefs, fig. 73.
Four Saints, fig. 74, 75.
St. Leonard (St. Laurence), pl. 88–89.
Bronze doors, pl. 90–94 ; fig. 112.
The two Pulpits, figs. 125–131 ; pl. 141–149.

FLORENCE, S. MARIA NOVELLA.
(Marzocco, pl. 16, 17).

FLORENCE, OGNISSANTI.
(St. Rossore, fig. 24).

FLORENCE, OR SAN MICHELE.
St. Mark, pl. 7–8 ; fig. 7.
St. Peter, fig. 6.
St. George, pl. 13–15 ; fig. 11.
The Tabernacle of the Parte Guelfa, fig. 21.
(St. Louis, pl. 31–33).

FLORENCE, FRONT OF PALAZZO VECCHIO.
Judith and Holofernes, pl. 124–127 ; figs. 117–119.

FLORENCE, LOGGIA DEI LANZI.
(Judith, pl. 124–127 ; figs. 117–119).

FLORENCE, VIA PIETRA PIANA.
Madonna Relief, fig. 156.

FLORENCE, MERCATO VECCHIO.
(Dovizia, fig. 44).

FLORENCE, PALAZZO MEDICI.
(Bronze David, pl. 66–69).
Eight Medallions, fig. 80.
(Judith, pl. 124–127).
(Marsyas, fig. 167).

FLORENCE, CASA MARTELLI.
The Martelli Shield, fig. 14.
(John the Baptist, pl. 59–64).
(David, fig. 65).

FLORENCE, MUSEO NAZIONALE (Bargello).
David, pl. 1–6.
St. George, pl. 13–15.
The Marzocco, pl. 16, 17.
Putto, pl. 40.
So-called Atys, pl. 41–43.
Niccolò da Uzzano, fig. 48 ; pl. 53.

FLORENCE, Museo Nazionale (Bargello)—*continued*.
    Two bronze busts, figs. 45, 46.
    St. John Relief, fig. 47.
    Bronze David, pl. 66–69.
    Decorative Head, pl. 136.
    Crucifixion, pl. 138.
    Stucco Reliefs, pl. 139, 140 ; fig. 112.
    Plaquette, fig. 139.

FLORENCE, Uffizi.
    Marsyas (restored), fig. 167.

LILLE, Musée Wicar.
    Dance of Salome, pl. 71.

LONDON, Victoria & Albert Museum.
    St. George and the Dragon, fig. 12.
    Cupid with a Fish, fig. 38.
    Christ in the Sepulchre, fig. 56.
    St. Peter Relief, pl. 72, 73.
    St. Cecilia, fig. 78.
    Pietà, pl. 137.
    Forzore Altar, fig. 111.
    Martelli Mirror, fig. 122.
    Plaquette, fig. 138.
    Nativity, fig. 145.
    Madonna Reliefs, figs. 148, 153, 158, 160.

LONDON, Wallace Coll.
    Plaquette, fig. 142.

NAPLES, San Angelo a Nilo.
    Tomb of Cardinal Brancacci, fig. 27 ; pl. 70.

PADUA, S. Antonio.
    High Altar, figs. 82, 83.
    Christ in the Sepulchre, fig. 55 ; pl. 113, 114.
    Crucifix, fig. 81 ; pl. 115.
    The Evangelist Symbols, pl. 95–98.
    The four Miracle Reliefs, pl. 99–109.
    Entombment, pl. 110–112.
    Madonna, fig. 93 ; pl. 116.
    The four Saints, fig. 90.
    St. Francis, pl 117, 119.
    St. Louis and St. Prosdocimus, figs. 99, 100.
    Angel Reliefs, fig. 95.
    Sportello, fig. 96.

PADUA, Front of S. Antonio.
    Monument of Gattamelata, fig. 105 ; pl. 120–123.

PARIS, Louvre.
    John the Baptist, fig. 23.
    Portrait of a Boy, Relief, fig. 47A.
    David, fig. 67.
    Crucifixion, fig. 124.
    Scourging of Christ, fig. 135.
    Plaquettes, figs. 141, 143.
    Madonna Reliefs, figs. 146, 150, 163.

PARIS, Musée Jacquemart-André.
    Putto as candle-holder, fig. 40.
    Lodovico Gonzaga, fig. 101.
    St. Sebastian, fig. 123.

PHILADELPHIA, Joseph E. Widener.
    Cupid, fig. 39.
    David, fig. 65.

PISA, S. Stefano.
    St. Rossore, fig. 24.

PRATO, Duomo.
    Pulpit, figs. 63, 64, 114.

ROME, Church of Ara Coeli.
    Tomb of Giovanni Crivelli, fig. 30.

ROME, San Giovanni in Laterano.
    Tomb of Pope Martin V, fig. 32 ; pl. 65.

ROME, St. Peter's.
    Tabernacle, fig. 51 ; pl. 74–78.

SIENA, Cathedral.
    Tomb of Bishop Giovanni Pecci, fig. 29 ; pl. 34.
    John the Evangelist, pl. 129, 133–135.
    Madonna Relief, fig. 165.

SIENA, Baptistery, Baptismal Font.
    Dance of Salome, pl. 35, 36.
    Faith, pl. 37.
    Hope, pl. 38.
    Putti, pl. 39 (40) ; figs. 35, 37, (36).

TURIN, Armeria.
    Sword hilt, fig. 121.

VENICE, S. Maria Gloriosa dei Frari.
    John the Baptist, fig. 109.

The Holy Trinity.   Detail from Fig. 21